PRACTICAL VEGAN

How to save Earth and Nourish Ourselves

Veggie Slayer Press

Beth Montgomery

Susan Rooker

All Rights Reserved
Printed in the United States of America
First Edition

For information about permission to reproduce selections of
this book or special discounts for bulk purchase, please contact
practicalvegan@gmail.com

Cover Art and photographs by WomanSong Studio

Library of Congress Cataloging-in-Publication Data

Montgomery, Beth
Rooker, Susan
Practical Vegan: How to Save Earth and Nourish Ourselves/
Montgomery, Rooker – 1st ed/
ISBN: 978-0-578-04110-0

PRACTICAL VEGAN

ACKNOWLEDGMENTS

Susan: This book would never have been completed without the love and support of my husband, David and sons, Ben and Max. I both love and admire you. A big thank you.

Thanks to T-bone and Halley, my canine constant companions while I typed away.

Another big thank you to the vegans, vegan writers, and activist, past and present, who have blazed a trail or swapped a recipe so that others, like me, can venture forth with more ease

Beth: I give a big "thank you"
-To my Lord and Creator God for His blessings

-The love of my life and our wonderful sons for all your support and enthusiasm.

-And to you the reader, for being interested in your health and our world and trusting this book is a good starting place

* * * * * * *

PRACTICAL VEGAN

CONTENTS

PREFACE

Perhaps you are ready to make a change or have made a change and need a little more to keep you going. *Practical Vegan* will give you the tools to do it. The effects of veganism, personally and globally, are great. You may already have a hint of that. Guess what? Your journey is just as important as the destination.

As we made the transition to veganism, we found great support and encouragement in each other and realized than many people didn't have the same. As we worked through challenges on our journey, we found many common obstacles both for "seasoned" vegans face as well as people transitioning to veganism. Some common questions are "why vegan?". I'm just one person, what good will it do? How can I be vegan when your family is not.

It doesn't take long down the vegan path before one runs into an all or nothing mentality. It goes something like this:

You have to be perfectly vegan in all areas - what you are eating, wearing, and thinking or you are not vegan at ALL and possibly even a hypocrite. This is destructive and does not take into consideration how much even a small change affects the lives of the animals, the environment, or our own health.

This book was written for those who are interested in making a change or simply ask the question "why vegan"?

Vegan: As defined by The Vegan Society, founded by Donald Watson, in 1944, "the word "veganism" denotes a philosophy and way of living which seeks to exclude all products derived wholly or partly from animals " — as far as is possible and practical [1]

Practical Vegan will encourage and enable you to be vegan as much as it is practical in your life. Every bit counts.

{A note about this book: To avoid the "who wrote this part" conundrum, we've opted to go with the ubiquitous 'we'. Where you read 'we', assume that we are referring to Beth and Susan as a unit. However, in specific situations that will be obvious to you, we have chosen to maintain our identities.}

- *Beth & Susan*
  Old Orchard Beach, Maine
  October 2009

---

[1] The Vegan News, The Company Acts 1944-1976, Memorandum of Association of The Vegan Society, pp1.

1. BIG PICTURE

The earth we abuse and the living things we kill will, in the end, take their revenge; for in exploiting their presence we are diminishing our future. ~*Marya Mannes, More in Anger, 1958*

Ham, bacon, steak , a nugget, a finger, a tender. Broil it. Fry it. Roast it. Skewer, sauté, au jus it. Fricassee, stuff, or tartar it. Where does it come from and what's really in it? To uncover the answers is to open yourself and develop awareness of the Western diet's influences our environment.

But wait! What about the animals? Ya know – the animals whose lives are created only to be sliced, diced, minced, and succotashed. Yes, their existence is the reason for this contamination. Descriptions of their lives are applicable and, though we may sidle up to the topics of rights, there will be little discussion here. In *Practical Vegan*, the focus is saving our planet.

We need to eat. Obviously. We are humans, the deciders. We decide who will live and who will die. Oftentimes, even how. We even decide who eats and who starves. Millions of people (about 1.2 billion according to The World Health

3

Organization)[2] have few choices of what they eat, if anything, due to circumstances beyond their control. Others have more choices though choose the least expensive and least healthy.

Still there are some who, with practically limitless culinary options at their disposal, choose to consume the most environmentally toxic food, namely meat, eggs, dairy, and yes, even fish.

"Exaggeration" you say? Hyperbole for the sake of selling a book? A load of crap? Ahhh – now you're getting warm.

Where The Domestic Things Are

More often, on today's packaging for meat, dairy and eggs, there is little visual connection between the contents and the source. For instance, on much of Hood's milk, there are no photos or drawings of cows. (Chocolate milk is an exception where a cartoon brown and white cow, on 2 legs, hands over a glass of chocolate milk while donning sunglasses.) Eggland's Best eggs have no images of hens on their packaging. Other egg packaging has only images of farms, wheat, or an unknown grain.

Colorful, cute drawings and photos on packaging of dairy, eggs, and meat may give the appearance that what you are purchasing from a supermarket or large health food stores is from a picturesque, family-owned, bucolic farm. There, just over the sun drenched rolling green hills, cows freely and happily giving over their milk, pastured chickens smile as you ever-so-carefully put their freshly layed eggs into a wicker basket and where plump pink pigs rejoice at going to slaughter to provide you with pork products.

---

[2] http://www.who.int/hdp/poverty/en/

More and more, as family farms struggle to exist, these images are largely fantasy. The majority of animal -based products sold today are from creatures who barely see grass, let alone scratching at the ground or rooting in dirt. For many, the only glimpse of sun they get is on the way to the slaughterhouse.

And, as you might have guessed, these animals do not have a home on the range. Their fattened, shortened lives are spent in cramped pens, cages, or small 30" x 72" crates (for the many unfortunate male calves)[3]. With larger "farms" comes larger amounts of, well, let's just call it pollution. Toxic, smelly, pollution of all kinds.

Now we're getting closer to that "load of crap".

[3] "Veal, a Byproduct of the Cruel Dairy industry",
http://origin.www.peta.org/mc/factsheet_display.asp?ID=102

2. WHY BE VEGAN: BETH

So Why Be Vegan?

Yes, why be vegan, why bother? Why be a minority of a minority? Here are a few of our answers:

Stewardship: The United States could feed so many more people! *"If in the land we currently use to grow grain for the livestock in the US was used to grow grain edible for human consumption, the number of people who could be fed would be nearly 800 million"* [4]

Is it right to indulge in a "luxury" such as eating flesh when abstaining from it could help feed so many starving people? I don't feel deprived at all on a vegan diet. Rather, I feel invigorated! Also, I came to consider eating a cow rather like eating a puppy. GROSS. If I look in both of their eyes and I don't see the difference between them.

In the West, most humans do not need to kill animals to survive. Instead, we can actually feed far more people by **not** killing animals (and breeding them in the first place). Survival does not depend on consuming flesh. Statistics show that a

[4]Cornell Science News, August 7, 1997.
http://www.news.cornell.edu/releases/aug97/livestock.hrs.html

balanced vegan diet will improve our health and survival. [5].

The animal agriculture industry is cruel. Much of organic (animal) farming is not different than the mainstream agriculture. Chickens live in filth, crammed together and are mistreated, neglected and debeaked without pain killers. Cows are kept impregnated for their milk. Male calves are taken away right after birth to be kept in a pen so small they cannot turn or move so they can be turned into veal. The mother mourns for not being able to care for her baby. Abuse and infections are rampant. Pigs, according to researchers at Penn State can learn "many of the same tasks we ask other animals to do"[6] are severely mistreated and abused. I do not want to be a part of this cycle. God gave man dominion over the earth and it's creatures and I will not be part of an abuse cycle.

Saving Lives: Because you can save approx. 100 animals a year by adopting a vegan lifestyle.

Mental Health: Many medical reports state that people feel better on a healthy vegetarian diet.

Beth is a _Practical vegan_. What does that mean for her?

1.   It means that I do whatever I can to avoid consuming or using animal products.

2.   It means that while practical veganism is one of the ways I try to honor God, it is NOT my religion, nor is it my "god" and I do not serve veganism. Rather, it serves me.

---

[5] http://www.pcrm.org/health/veginfo/vegetarian_foods.html
[6] http://www.rps.psu.edu/probing/pigs.html

3. It means that I will do everything I can to get clothing products like shoes, made out of man-made materials, even when it means ordering online, returning and re-ordering. But since I have a back and foot problem (even with professional orthotics), I must wear very supportive shoes. From time to time, I need more selection then is available to me in man-made material. Sometimes I don't have the means to do that or just need a store to try them on. If a pair or two of my shoes are made in part with leather, then they are leather. I've done what I could to avoid it, but it does not make me a "non-vegan".

Also, I have a medical condition that requires that I take a medicine that has an animal derivative in it. To date, there are no substitutes that work as well. I have tried. Believe me – I have tried! I take this medicine I need to stay well and be able to function. Practical veganism *makes the effort* to try to do no harm, but veganism is a journey and a mode of heart and philosophy – not a destination, not an elite social club and certainly *not* a religion.

4. The International Vegan Union states, "Membership in the Society is available to all who wish to see the object achieved and who undertake to live as closely to the ideal as personal circumstances permit" I take the latter part seriously. Veganism is not about torturing oneself! To me, being vegan is about caring for oneself by taking care of the body God gave me, eating the diet He originally laid out, and caring for the world in which we live.[7]

---

[7]Bible; 1 Corinthians 6:19,Genesis 1:26,Genesis 1:29)

The Vegan Outreach website states,

> "Some vegans claim sugar (and vegan products containing sugar, like Tofutti) isn't vegan because some sugar processing uses bone char as a whitening agent. Bone char (a granular material that is produced from the burning of animal bones) is also used as a source of activated carbon in some water filters and by some municipal water treatment plants. (These plants also use tests that involve animal products, and water itself has been tested on animals.) So should we say *water* isn't vegan?

The way veganism is presented to a potential vegan is of major importance. The attractive idea behind being a "vegan" is reducing one's contribution to animal exploitation. Buying meat, eggs, and/or dairy creates animal suffering–animals will be raised and slaughtered specifically for these products. But if the by-products are not sold, they will be thrown out or given away. As more people stop eating animals, the by-products will naturally fade, so there is no real reason to force other people to worry about them in order to call themselves "vegan."

"A vegan world, not a vegan club."

This is the philosophy I hold.

How I got here:

My journey started slowly. Ironically, it was the inhumane treatment to animals that made me begin on this journey, and it is stewardship as well as health that keeps me here.

At about 12 years old, I learned how the calves were treated that veal was made out of. How they were never allowed to walk but tied down in a small pen, not even being able to turn so they would not get muscle and be tender. From then on I refused to eat veal. I wrongly assumed that this was an isolated incident and all the rest of the animals lived healthy and happy lives...well - until they ended up on my plate. But by that time, they were so far removed and looked so different from what they once were, that there was a disconnect in my brain.

Around 19, I began going for months at a time without eating any meat because meat bored me. I just got tired of it. About a year later, I watched a video like PETA's "Meet your Meat" that opened my eyes to the inhumane and cruel treatment of animals bred for food and went fully vegetarian.

My adult life has been characterized by long, long bouts of vegetarianism or veganism only broken up by periods of eating meat when my health would decline as a vegetarian because my B12 was not absorbing. I didn't know the cause at the time, but now I have found the importance of a good B12 vitamin! I have also found the place in my life where health and ideals meet - and for me it is <u>practical veganism</u>.

When I eat a balanced vegetarian based diet, I feel better physically and emotionally. Emotionally because I am not contributing to cruelty of animals, and physically because I have more energy, my weight is lower, my steps are lighter, my outlook brighter.

I love the diverse vegetarian foods, the tastes, textures, colors and spices. A vegetarian easily draws from many cultures foods and spices. Such cuisines include those from India, China, The Middle-East as well as Central and South America and utilize spices indigenous to those regions. I enjoy cooking and love the smell and the comfort of a good vegetarian meal. I also tend to be drawn to other vegetarians. Over all they are a warm, caring and compassionate group of people that I enjoy sharing life with. An example of this is my dear friend and co-author Susan who has a deep compassion for both animals and humanity.

(A note on religions and Veganism: Beth is a Christian vegan, and many people ask why (and how) she is a both Christian and a vegan. They are not mutually exclusive! Actually she considers veganism one way she can honor God by doing her part to take care of the world He entrusted to her. Some religions are naturally vegetarian, like the Buddhists or 7th Day Adventists. Some are not. Regardless of your ideology, you can be a vegan! Most belief systems applaud taking care of yourself as well as the things around you.)

Some "Right now" resources:

www.veganoutreach.org/whyvegan/WhyVegan.pdf
www.vegan.org/about_veganism/index.html
www.news.cornell.edu/releases/aug97/livestock.hrs.html
www.ivu.org/history/world-forum/1951vegan.html
http://earthfirst.com
Physicians Committee for Responsible Medicine
(http://www.pcrm.org)

3. AIR

"Complaints about the smell of our factory farms, and only the smell, are the final insult...We notice these places, many of us, only when the odors reach our homes and new subdivisions, affecting our own quality of life. We create these animals for our profit and pleasure, playing with their genes, violating their dignity as living creatures, forcing them to lie and live in their own urine and excrement, turning pens into penitentiaries and frustrating their every desire except what is needed to keep them breathing and breeding. And then we complain about the smell."

-- *Matthew Scully, author of Dominion: The Power of Men, the Suffering of Animals, and the Call to Mercy*

Let's go on an adventure. First, to a rural small farm. We're standing a few yards away from a beautiful bucolic scene. Horses neighing. Cows mooing. Every once in a while, we hear the bleating of a sheep calling to its lamb. Rolling hills, waving wheat, and the earthy smell of manure, drying in the afternoon sun, ready to fertilize growing seedlings.

Next on our little journey, we'll head to a Concentrated Animal Feeding Operation (CAFO). A CAFO is an animal feeding operation in which "1) animals have been, are, or will be stabled or confined and fed or maintained for a total of 45 days or more in any 12-month period and 2), crops, vegetation, forage growth, or post-harvest residues are *not* sustained over any portion of the operation lot or facility." Our noses will know we're arriving long before we see it.

Now we're standing a few yards away from the CAFO. This is 'home' to close to 20,000 hogs crammed in long pens or, if they are females, they may be standing (because they have not space to sit) in a gestation crate. Each hog generates 2.5 times the amount of poop and urine as one person.[8] The pigs stand on slats and their waste drops to a pit. The pit is occasionally flushed out and its contents are pumped into an open air holding "pond". This reservoir, 30 feet deep in some places, is pink, not brown. The pink color comes from a mixture of (hold on to your cookies) blood, afterbirth, and stillborn piglets along with the pee and poop.[9]

---

[8] Justine, Thompson, Transcript of Lecture, http://www.law.mercer.edu/elaw/jthompson.htm
[9] Jeff Tietz, Rolling Stones, December 14, 2006, *Boss Hog*

CAFO Parameters*

	Small	Medium	Large
Cows	Less than 300	300-999	1000+
Swine (under 55 lbs)	Less than 3,000	3,000-9,999	10,000+
Swine (over 55 lbs)	Less than 750	750-2,499	2500+
Turkeys	less than 16,500	16,500 - 54,999	55,000+
Hens (Layers or broilers)	Less than 25,000	25,000-81,999	82,000+
Chickens (Other than laying hens)	less than 37,500	37,500 - 124,999	125,000+
Ducks	Less than 10,000	10,000-29,999	30,000+

*Data based on United States Department of Environmental Protection's *"Regulatory Definitions of Large CAFOs, Medium CAFOs, Small CAFOs"*

According to Dr. Michael Greger, director of public health and agriculture at the US Humane Society, "Pig waste lagoons are a great danger to human health. There are many ways - the wind for example – that illness can be spread from them.' [10] In Iowa, "where the 20 million hogs easily outnumber the 3 million people, the rotten-egg-and-ammonia smell of hog waste often wafts into homes, landing like a punch to the

---

[10] Sharon Churcher, The Mail Online, May 3, 2009, *The Smell is so awful that I start to vomit: Is this the farm of Ground Zero of Swine Flu?*

chest."[11] "Pig manure contains such concentrated chemicals as ammonia, nitrogen, sulfites and phosphorus."[12]

The stench is oppressive. Our eyes tear, burn. This is no place we want to stay, let alone visit again.

An average swine lagoon of pink glop contains harmful gases such as:

- methane,
- sulfur containing compounds (hydrogen sulfide, dimethyl sulfide)
- nitrogen containing compounds (ammonia, methylamines, skatoles –which helps provide the lovely aroma of poop, and indoles.)
- carbon monoxide,
- cyanide

excess nutrients:
- phosphorous,
- potassium

heavy metals:
- nitrates
- arsenic (mixed in with chicken and pig feed; according to scientists at the non-profit, independent institution Marine Biological Laboratory (MBL) and Dartmouth School of Medicine, "the ability to mount an immune response to influenza A (H1N1) infection is significantly compromised by a low level of arsenic exposure that commonly occurs through drinking contaminated well water"[13]
- copper

[11] http://www.azstarnet.com/sn/news/283076.php
[12] Danit Lidor, http://www.wired.com/ Big Stink Over a Pig, 07.01.02
[13] *Scientists Link Influenza A (H1N1) Susceptibility to Common Levels of Arsenic Exposure*, Press Release, May 20, 2009

- selenium,
- zinc
- cadmium
- molybdenum
- nickel
- lead
- iron,
- manganese,
- aluminum
- boron

as well as more than *100* microbial pathogens including
- Salmonella: microscopic little buggers that pass from the feces of animals and people to other animals and people[14]
- Campylobacter: According to the Center for Disease Control (CDC) it one of most common causes of diarrhea[15]
- Escherichia coli: E. Coli was responsible for 7 food borne outbreaks between September 2006 and July 2009[16]
- Cryptosporidium: commonly known as "crypto", produces cramps and diarrhea)
- Listeria monocytogenes: causes nearly 2,500 cases of listeriosis per year in the United States. It primarily affects pregnant women, newborns, and adults with weakened immune systems[17]
- Cryptosporidium (C. parvum): causes abdominal pain, profuse diarrhea, weight loss, loss of appetite and anorexia, but in otherwise healthy individuals the

[14] http://www.cdc.gov/nczved/dfbmd/disease_listing/salmonellosis_gi.html
[15] http://www.cdc.gov/nczved/dfbmd/disease_listing/campylobacter_gi.html
[16] http://www.cdc.gov/ecoli/2009/0701.htm
[17] http://www.cdc.gov/pulsenet

infection is usually self-limiting and resolves within a few weeks[18]
- streptocolli
- girardia. (Each gram of hog poo can contain as much as 100 million fecal coliform bacteria.

organic acids which include
- acetic acid
- butyric acids
- valeric acids
- caproic acids
- propanoic acid.[19]

And at least eleven antibacterial or antifungal compounds or groups of compounds that are widely used in swine feeds. [20]
Consider this, Faculty Emeritus, John Kirk DVM, MPVM, MS of Dairy Health and Food Safety at UC Davis' School of Veterinary Medicine states in his report *"Pathogens in Manure – Strategies to Prevent Infections"*,

"Dairymen should use any strategy that will break this cycle of spread. Controlling these animal diseases will also help to reduce the hazard of market cows going to slaughter with potential human foodborne pathogens."

That's to just to *REDUCE* the hazard? This ignores the presence and hazard of the pathogens getting into the soil, water, and air in the first place.

---

[18] Soave R. *Human Coccidian Infections*. IN Tropical and Geographical Medicine, Mahmoud AAF and Warren KS, eds., 1994 as sited in www.cdfound.to.it
[19] http://www.pewtrusts.org/news_room_detail.aspx?id=38438

[20]Marcia S. Carlson, Thomas J. Fangman. Department of Animal Sciences, University of Missouri, Extension, *Swine Antibiotics and Feed Additives*, Jan 2009,

According to the CDC (Center for Disease Control), there are over 200 food-related illnesses and many of these, including *Campylobacter jejuni, E. Coli, Listeria monocytogenes, Cyclospora cayetanensis* were not even recognized as causes of foodborne illness 20 years ago.

Since just 2008, the United States Department of Agriculture has recalled **over 150MILLION pounds of meat and meat products**. (See Appendix for detailed breakdown). However, this includes ***only US recalls*** and does not include the almost 1.5 million sheep and cattle (not pounds or kilograms but actual *living, breathing animals*) slaughtered and burned in Britain's 2001 Foot and Mouth scare, 4,383 cattle in China in 2005,[21] or the over 4.7 million animals slaughtered in Britain in over a 6 year period (about 15,000 per week) in the 1990s[22].

1997 Bird flu: 1.5 million chickens killed in Hong Kong[23], 2004/5: Vietnam: 66 million birds[24], 17 million birds in British Colombia. [25]

Even if you saw animals as simply "food" or "protein", you might still recognize this as unfathomable waste, aside how they lived.

---

[21] "1000 Birds Killed in China's Avian Flu Outbreak" Daily News Central, Health News, May 27, 2005

[22] "EU Approves Plan to Slaughter British Cows" Daily News, April 3, 1996

[23] http://www.dhhs.state.nh.us/DHHS/CDCS/Avian+Flu/default.htm

[24] Vietnam, South Korea, Nigeria battle avian flu
Dec 22, 2006 Center For Infectious Disease Research and Policy, University of Minnesota,

[25] Avian Flu, the Next Pandemic? May 12, 2008 .www.cbc.ca.

More Public "Health"

It's one thing to read and imagine what it might be like to visit one of these sites. It is very different to live nearby. The neighbors of CAFOs have, in comparison to those of us who do not live anywhere near them, a poorer quality of life, poorer heath and, poorer property value.

First, there's the odor. There are so many compounds that emanate from the livestock, specifically their manure, that not just one of them is responsible for the smell. Think of a symphony...all the instruments working together to make a magnificent moving piece of music. One of the gases emitted from CAFOs is hydrogen sulfide, perhaps better known as "sewer gas". Sulfide –as in 'sulfur' and the small of rotten eggs. It doesn't take much of this gas to funk up a square mile.

Neighbors of CAFOs (swine, poultry, cattle) demonstrate a higher level of respiratory and neurological problems. Hydrogen sulfide, says Dr. Kaye Kilburn, professor at the University of Southern California and expert on H_2S and its effects on the body, should be avoided everywhere.

Dr. Susan S. Schiffmann from Duke University, says that "persons living near the intensive swine operations who experienced the odors reported significantly more tension, more depression, more anger, less vigor, more fatigue, and more confusion than control subjects" as measured by the a psychological assessment called POMS (Profile of Mood States). [26]

People living near industrial swine operations are very often unable to open their windows or even go outside and experience increased occurrences of headaches, runny nose,

---

[26] *Brain Research Bulletin, Volume 37, Issue 4, 1995, Pages 369-375 The effect of environmental odors emanating from commercial swine operations on the mood of nearby residents, by Dr. Susan Shiffmann et al*

sore throat, excessive coughing, diarrhea, and burning eyes as compared to residents of the community with no intensive livestock operations.[27] Children and the elderly are most vulnerable to chronic lung and heart disorders.[28]

Yet another study in the Journal of Agricultural Health and Safety states that neighbors (up to 2 miles away) of a 40,000 swine containment facility demonstrated a "significantly higher rates of four clusters of symptoms known to represent toxic or inflammatory effects on the respiratory tract."

And if you think "not in my backyard", you may want to rethink that. With little fanfare, a farm in Tewksbury, Massachusetts, allegedly violated building codes, and built "a 10,000 square foot finisher building, for confining hogs, with a 500,000 gallon waste storage tank below"[29]. The family run pig farm, in existence since the '40s changed their operations by adding pigs in a confined area. "We have no issue with the farmers," says one neighbor" but the smell is just awful. It makes our eyes water and we can't even go outside." Residential homes are less than 600 feet away[30], just a little over an NFL football field away from 500-2500 pigs (The farmers were unable to provide an exact number to me, citing the Federal Bio Securities laws.)

Delightful.

---

[27] Steve Wing, Suzanne Wolf, Environmental Health Perspectives, Volume 108, Number 3, March 2000,

[28] " PEW Commission says Industrial Scale Farm Animals Production Poses "Unacceptable" Risks to Public Health, Environment", PEW Charitable Trust Press Release, April 29, 2008.

[29] www.tewskburyodor.org/aboutus.html

[30] www.tewksburyodor.org

Employees

Can you imagine WORKING in these environments? There is much more documentation relating to those who work in CAFOs. *Common* health complaints among these workers include

- sinusitis,
- chronic bronchitis
- nasal mucous membrane inflammation,
- nasal and throat irritation,
- headaches and muscle aches and pains (University of Iowa Study Group 2002).
- decreased lung abilities

And this does not include those who lost fingers, legs, arms or Life due to the machinery, spillage, or storage..

Environmental Health

Certainly by now, you've heard about global warming or climate change. You may believe it exists, is caused or exacerbated by human activity. You may even be skeptical of the entire (or parts of the) theory. You may believe the projections that our planet may warm another 1.4°C – to 5.8° by 2100, larger than "any century long trend in the last 10,000 years".[31] Or not.

Either way, that's fine with us. In writing this book, we are not aiming to make a believer out of you. No. Instead, we hope that by providing well-researched and well- documented data, you are better able to decide – FOR YOURSELF- if eating

---

[31] *Livestock's Long Shadow-Environmental Issues and Options,* Food and Agriculture Organization of The United Nations, November 2006, p. 80.

today's meat and its accompanying industrial complex is, well, worth it.

Which is worse for our environment? Driving a car or eating a burger? You certainly know by now that those gas guzzlers, tractor trailers and jet airplanes are no friends to the environment. You may not know there is a little dirty secret that the meat industry prefers you not know, that the raising and distribution of livestock is the number one cause of greenhouse gases. Two of these gases, methane (CH_4) and nitrous oxide (N_2O), are more potent than the more commonly feared carbon dioxide (CO_2).

Greenhouse Effect

The Greenhouse Effect keeps our planet warm. This is a good thing. The sun's rays bounce off the Earth's atmosphere, are lost in outer space, or are absorbed by and warm Earth. In turn, when the Earth is warmed, it radiates its own heat. This heat, known as infrared rays, then bounces back into outer space or absorbed by several gases (greenhouse gases) in Earth's atmosphere. These include but are not limited to water vapor, carbon dioxide, nitrous oxide, ozone and methane.

Without these greenhouse gases, heat would escape back into space and Earth would be much colder, on average 60°F colder. Of this, there is little debate. This is measurable. However, an over abundance of these same gases means that even LESS heat is allowed to escape into space, thereby warming the Earth further.

Measuring Greenhouse gases

In order for anything to be measured, it needs to be compared to something everyone agrees on (like the size of an inch, a gallon, or a decibel.) When measuring greenhouse gases they are compared to something everyone knows - carbon dioxide. So, the measurement, the Global Warming Potential (GWP), measures how much heat *one molecule* of a certain gas will trap relative to *one molecule* of carbon dioxide. The GWP of CO2 is 1. Methane has a GWP of 23, which means it is 23 times more effective at preventing infrared radiation from escaping the planet. [32]

According to the UN's report, *Livestock's Long Shadow,* 18% of CO2 equivalent greenhouse gases is from livestock, its feeding, processing, and transporting. More than caused by all of transportation. Each kilogram of beef (2.2 lbs) generates 50 kilograms or greenhouse gases versus driving one kilometer (.62 miles) in a car that generates only ½ kilogram of greenhouse gases.[33]

YES! Eating meat generates more greenhouse gases then driving a car. So if you ate, say 6 servings of 6oz a week, (most restaurant servings range from 6oz-9oz and even 16oz pieces[34]) and drove 50 miles in one week, (80.5 kilometers) you would have generated (40.25 kilograms from the driving and 50 kilograms of greenhouse gases from the meat. If you are a meat eater, you likely eat more than that and you likely drive more than 50 miles a week. Note that this does not include air travel.)

---

[32] *Livestock's Long Shadow-Environmental Issues and Options,* Food and Agriculture Organization of The United Nations, November 2006, p. 82, Table 3-1, *Past and current concentration of important greenhouse gases.*
[33]" Global Warming, Cool It!," Travel, *Australian Greenhouse Office, Department of the Environment and Water Resources, 2007*
http://www.environment.gov.au/settlements/gwci/transport.html
[34] Longhorn Steakhouse menu, www.longhornsteakhouse.com.

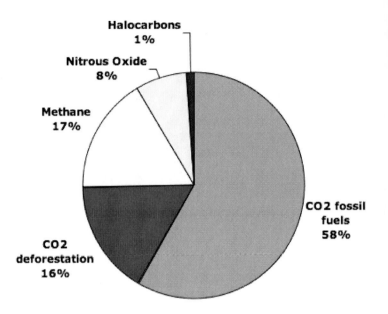

Source: Intergovernmental Panel on Climate Change (IPCC) 2007

Carbon Dioxide (CO₂)

No question about it. Carbon dioxide (CO2) is a major contributing gas to the warming of our planet. CO2 is both naturally generated (volcanic eruption, plant/animal decay, permafrost melting to release trapped carbon) and human created (burning of fossil fuels, e.g.).

According to the UN report, "between 25 and 30 percent of the greenhouse gases released into the atmosphere each year is caused by deforestation, 80 percent of which is due to increased farmland to feed growing populations." (United Nations Food and Agriculture Organization (FAO) October 2006).

24

As countries grow richer and the demand for meat increases, so will the need for more land on which to grow cereal for these animals to consume. Between 40and 50% of all grains are fed to livestock. Half of the world's entire wheat harvest goes to livestock and 75% of all soy is just for livestock, not humans. And get this, it takes 7 kilograms (about 15.5 lbs) of grain to make 1 kilogram (2.2 lbs) of meat[35]. Talk about inefficient.

Not impressed yet? How about this:

IF...all Americans (*just Americans*) ate meat:

One less day a week: This would result in the same carbon savings as taking 19.2 million cars off the road in the USA for one year. Equal to save 46 million return flights from New York to Los Angeles and back from Los Angeles to New York.

Two less days a week: This would result in the same carbon savings as replacing ALL household appliances in the US with energy efficient ones.

Three less days a week: This would have a greater impact on the climate than replacing all US cars with Toyota Prius models.

Four less days a week: Same as halving the domestic use of all electricity, gas, oil, petroleum and kerosene in the United States.
(Are you getting the picture?)
Five less days a week (or eating meat only on weekends): would equal planting 13 billion trees in your garden letting them grow for ten years. That is 43 trees per American!

Six less days a week: Same as eliminating the total electricity use of all households in the United States.

---

[35] Dr. Harry Aiking, Transcript, "Meat The Truth", Nicolaas G. Pierson Foundation.

If everyone in the United States ate a vegetarian diet for seven days, they would save around just the same removing *all of the cars in the USA* off the roads.[36]

Methane (N₂O)

Despite the fact that there is more CO2 than methane, methane may be more of a contributor to greenhouse gases than previously thought. According to Drew Shindell at NASA's Goodard Institute, the impacts of methane on climate warming may be double the standard amount attributed to the gas[37]

Methane is largely generated by cows and sheep at the end of the digestive process. These livestock along with deer, elk, bison that are often raised for food, have a complex digestive system, much more so then humans. They can digest plant fibers where as humans cannot.

As the cows chews and swallow the grasses, it travels into one of its four stomachs where it is mixed with saliva and a cocktail of bacteria, fungi, and protozoa. These microorganisms break down and ferment the plants. It is regurgitated (the cud). And the cow takes another chomp of grass. Methane is one of the end products of the rumen's process and is released by way of flatulence and belches.

Just flatulence or few burps? Not a big deal? Just how much? Well, the average dairy cow that produces 8,000-10,000 liters if milk a year will belch/toot out 500-700 liters of methane *a day*. That equals a large 4x4 vehicle traveling 35 miles every day.[38]

---

[36] Carbon Savings Table US, www.animalconcerns.org,

[37] *Methane's Impacts On Climate Change May Be Twice Previous Estimates*, http://www.sciencedaily.com/releases/2005/07/ 050718214744.htm

[38] Dr. David Davis, "Meat The Truth" Nicolaas G. Pierson Foundation, Transcript

When you consider that for each American there are three cows that burp and farm 24/7, combines with fact that livestock accounts for 60% of that country's methane emissions...there's a great deal we can do reduce these component of greenhouse gases. Namely, lay off the meat.

However, most of the meat sold in supermarkets today comes from livestock that were not fed grass but fed grain. Corn mostly. Some soy. Sweet juicy farm stand corn? No way. This corn is old and hard and starchy. Either way, sweet or hard, livestock cannot digest it. So why on earth would a farmer feed cows a food it couldn't digest? A food that causes bloating, gas, pain in the same cows whose sole purpose in life is to be killed? You already know the answer -money.

Corn is cheap. Thanks to government subsidies, it's really cheap. According to Independent Lens' film *King Corn*, "Between 2003 and 2005, for example, American taxpayers paid $34.75 billion in crop subsidy benefits to farmers, but only the top one percent of farmers received nearly one-fifth of that amount. In Iowa, 70 percent of subsidy payments go to only 20 percent of the state's commodity farmers." This corn, Yellow Dent, has a very thick outer skin that doesn't soften up to the point you can eat it even if you cook it for hours. [39] Also, called "dent corn" or "field corn", it is stored, delivered, and controlled much easier (and cheaper) than grass. Yellow Dent fattens livestock faster than grass and, as an added perk, the starches and sugars in the corn create fat. This fat creates the "marbleizing" effect that influences how the beef will be graded. "USDA Prime beef contains more fat marbling so it is the most tender and flavorful."[40]

If small amounts of grain are introduced, the cow can get by for a time. But when more amounts are fed to accelerate

---

[39] *Yellow Dent Corn*, http://waltonfeed.com/old/self/corn.html
[40] USDA, Food Safety and Inspection Service, *Beef...from Farm to Table*
http://www.fsis.usda.gov/Fact_Sheets/Beef_from_Farm_to_Table/index.asp

marblization or weight, the digestive system can't handle it and because grain is not digestible, gas builds and builds. Their stomachs bloat. Much more methane is released. One cow? No big deal...but 95 million...pee-yew (and those are just the cows).

An added issue is that this bloating causes stomach infections so, to combat THAT, you guessed it, antibiotics are mixed in the feed to slow down any infection. This leads to resistance to antibiotics which then encourages the growth of superbugs. Inevitable, cows, not 100% healthy, get into the food supply, not to mention the accompanying antibiotics. However, for our discussion here, let's stay focused on the environment.

Another way that raising livestock emits methane is in the management of the manure itself. Not only do the "lagoons" and holding tanks (also called "liquid manure management systems") pollute the groundwater, rivers, streams and eventually oceans, they can also cause a significant methane production. According to a US inventory report, methane emissions have continued to increase since 1990[41].

Methane, according to the International Emissions Trading Association, methane is 20 times more effective in trapping heat in the atmosphere than carbon dioxide (CO2).

---

[41]http://epa.gov/climatechange/emissions/downloads09/Agriculture.pdf

Table 1. Comparative Global Warming Potential (GWP) of Carbon Dioxide, Nitrous Oxide, and Methane. This is for a 100 year span. Note that these numbers raise when compared over only a 20 year span. GWP for Carbon Dioxide is always 1 because it is the gas being compared to. *(Data derived from 2007 Intergovernmental Panel on Climate Change (IPCC) Fourth Assessment Report)*

Greenhouse Gas	Lifetime (years)	GWP time horizon	
		20 years	100 years (What the Kyoto Protocol uses)
Carbon Dioxide (CO$_2$)	1	1	1
Methane (CH$_4$)	12	72	25
Nitrous oxide	114	289	298

According to G. Tyler Miller in *Sustaining The Earth: An Integrated Approach*, cattle belch methane accounts for 16% of the world's annual methane missions to the atmosphere.[42]

---

[42] Miller, G. Tyler. *Sustaining the Earth: An Integrated Approach. U.S.A.: Thomson Advantage Books, 2007.* 160.

In Canada, it is responsible for ¾ of all total methane, according to Environmental Canada.

In Australia, which has over 90 million sheep (about four sheep for every person) and 28 million cattle, the methane amount created is more warming than all of its coal-fired powered stations, producing 60% of all methane emissions.[43]

However, in the US, the EPA has established a voluntary outreach program to reduce methane emissions in the livestock industry. This program, known as the AgSTAR Program, encourages farms and farm factories of all sizes to adopt a "biogas recovery system" that will recover and burn methane or to make that gas available as energy for the farm/factory itself.[44] Also, recently, German scientists have developed a promising fist-size pill that, when mixed with a special diet and strict feeding times, may cut down on the livestock methane emissions. [45] This is *voluntary* and involves incurring expenses. No fines are levied if a farm or agribusiness does not step-up.

So, 20,000 years ago it was just the end of the last glaciation. Then, CO_2 concentration was quite low, at the order of 180 parts per million in the atmosphere. Then, because of natural processes, it rose to 280 parts per million, but this took several thousands of years. But now, during the last 200 years, it has risen by over 100 units, so as much as during the 10,000 years before. Agriculture is important,

---

[43] Geoff Russell, Barry Brook. *Meat's Carbon Hoofprint*, Australian Science, November/December 2007, p38.
[44] http://epa.gov/methane/sources.html
[45] Kate Connelley, "Pill stops cow burps and helps save the planet" .The Guardian, March 23, 2007

particularly for methane. If this can be reduced, it would be quite an efficient and cheap way to mitigate the global warming.   - *Dr. Jouni Raisanen, Climatologist from Helsinki University, Finland, Member of UN Intergovernmental Panel for Climate Change (IPCC)*

NITROUS OXIDE (N$_2$0)

Along with methane, nitrous oxide is a primary greenhouse case in agriculture, according the United States Environmental Protection Agency. It is also a by-product of, you guessed it, manure and urine management[46]. However, because most of farmed land generated food for the livestock, it is easy to see that we're it not for feeding these animals in the first place, much less N2O would be dispersed into the environment.

re of the less than that of agriculture as a whole. It is generated both naturally (bacterial break down in soil and oceans) and by humans. with a GWP of 310[47] is 310 times as effective as CO2 trapping heat in the atmosphere.[48] So a little goes a long way.

What to do?

You're reading this book so you already have a clue. The best thing you can do is, at the minimal, begin the road to veganism. Perhaps you prefer the "cold-turkey" approach, or even "whole hog"- to just clean out your kitchen, car and office of all products containing animals...even your leather chair.

---

[46] Executive Summary, 2009 U.S. Greenhouse Gas Inventory Report, April 2009, USEPA
[47] ibid
[48] ibid

Or, perhaps you take a practical vegan approach. Start. Just start. Do what is reasonable for you at this time. Each bit helps.

According to Dr. James Hansen, a leading climatologist and Director of the US Goddard Spaceflight Center, "there are many things that people can do to reduce their carbon emissions, but changing your light bulb and many of the things are much less effective than changing your diet because, if you eat further down on the food chain rather than animals which have produced many greenhouse gasses and used much energy in the process of growing that meat, you can actually make a bigger contribution in that way than just about anything."[49]

Stop eating animals and you use dramatically less fossil fuels, as much as 250 gallons less oil per year for vegans, says Cornell University's David Pimentel, and 160 gallons less for egg-and-cheese-eating vegetarians.[50]

---

[49] http://suprememastertv.com/bbs/board.php?bo_table=holidaycard&wr_id=141&goto_url=&url=link1_0
[50] Mike Tidwell, "The Low-Carbon Diet" Audubon Magazine, January-February 2009

4. WHY VEGAN: SUSAN

Fair Weather

My journey to being a Practical Vegan was a slow. No "Cold Turkey" for me. My adult life, that is, since going to college, has been speckled with sporadic stints of abstaining from consuming flesh.

As a fair-weather vegetarian, I would abstain from meat, sometimes only red meat, sometimes red meat and chicken and sometimes only eating tons of seafood and canned tuna. Always with dairy. Always with eggs.

It was no big deal to me to use products that contained ingredients from animal, such as marshmallows, (gelatin), soap (stearic acid), cake mixes (Sodium stearoyl lactylate) or even leather. After all, the animal was already dead. Wasn't using these products just helping to make sure that, ala Native American, nothing went to waste? Besides, what was the cow or chicken or fish or pig going to do, rise from the grave and say "Thanks, Susan!"? My meat-eating-vegetarian cycle became so commonplace that my youngest son, Max, would say "how long are you going to be a vegetarian this time?" He was right. It hadn't quite 'took'.

I would get an urge for blood and "indulge" in a slab of beef. A hunk of thick, juicy, medium-well flesh. After the first bite, a disconnected feeling infiltrated my being (along with the flood of saturated fat). At odds with my Self. I rationalized that I was a carnivore, eating meat was hardwired into my DNA, that I NEEDED beef, the protein, or iron it contained because my body was craving it. "Good for me" for "listening to my body." Besides, I was... Human, the top of the food chain, Ruler of all...an American, a woman, a mom, – anything to assuage that pesky "cat's-outta-the bag" part of me that knew, really knew what I was eating and how it got on my plate.

And I did know. I had read the books. I had watched documentaries and gruesome clips of undercover witnesses in the slaughterhouses. Audio books, YouTube clips, anything I could find. I intently listened to experts lecture on animal products', farm factories', and Concentrated Animal Feeding Operations' (CAFOs) contribution to the deterioration of our resources, planet and bodies. I understood.

In contrast, while in my vegetarian mode, I felt more in tune with the world around me and within. My cognitive dissonance, my unwelcomed feeling of eating animals that just didn't coincide with my belief, understanding that at some point, this flesh had been attached to a living, breathing, and feeling animal with eyes, a brain and a nervous system, vanished. I felt lighter, more grounded and connected....mostly. Yet, even in my "I'm a vegetarian but I each cheese and eggs" mode. I remained unsettled. Something still bugged me.

This cycle continued in various durations and incarnations for over 20 years. It wasn't until a few unrelated events occurred, did "it" click.

Sabbaticals, Qassams, and Pot-lucks

Like many cultures, food is important in getting Jews together. The pot-luck supper is the quintessential shared meal. Everyone brings a dish that is to be shared by all (until the good stuff runs out). I was always surprised that, the pot luck suppers, held and sponsored by the congregation of which I was a member, allowed meat. As a Reform Congregation, milk and meat could not be combined within the same dish but were allowed in separate dishes. I felt an uncomfortable disjoint between "tikon olum" repairing the world, as Jews are meant to do, and the consumption of today's meat. Disconnect.

First, in January 2008, the rabbi at the congregation of which I was a member, teacher and Member of the Board, went on sabbatical. Rabbi Joel Soffin schlepped up to Maine and led services, discussions and classes in her place. Rabbi Soffin, a life-long social activist, is a doer. I had never met a spiritual leader like him. Here was a man who lived as he spoke, who walked the walk. As the founder of Jewish Helping Hands/Yad Soffin Foundation, Rabbi Soffin has led trips to Rwanda, Cambodia, and Mexico to "tikon olam", repair the world. Rebuilding homes in New Orleans after Hurricane Katrina, building schools in Cambodia and restore a residential recovery facility for thirty women and their infant children are just a few of his many endeavors undertaken JHH (JFF, 2008)

And yet, it was important for him to meet the Congregation. Each board member invited he and his lovely wife to Shabbat dinner. He was personable and interested. He was interesting. He was vegetarian.

Secondly, before Israeli forces devastatingly attacked Gaza in December 2008, The World watched between 2001 and 2008, as "over 4048 rockets and 4040 mortars fired at Israeli targets" (www.mfa.gov, 2008). In December of '08, Israel, as expected, ferociously attacked Gaza in retaliation. According to the news service, JTA, *"The Research Department of the Israel Defense Intelligence identified 1,166 Palestinians killed during Israel's three-week military operation in Gaza. Of them, 709 were identified as operatives of Hamas or other terrorist*

groups and 295 were identified as "uninvolved Palestinians."
The IDF said another 162 had not yet been conclusively
identified one way or the other. Of the "uninvolved
Palestinians" killed, 89 were under the age of 16 and 49 were
women." (JTA, 2009)

Throughout the three week operation, I received
Facebook messages from "friends" reporting more qassam
rockets fired into Israel. I heard little fall-out from friends
(real, and virtual), leaders (Jewish or not) about the atrocity of
war. But for Jon Stewart from Comedy Central's *"The Daily
Show with Jon Stewart"*, I heard no Jewish dissent. Was it
wrong, un-American, or (dare I say) un-Jewish to disagree with
the harm being inflicted on Palestinians?

Perhaps The World was distracted by the upcoming
inauguration of our first black American president. Perhaps
American were rationalizing that "Palestinians had it coming to
them" or that it was not our problem. Either way, my
observation was that they were disconnected, in denial, and
apathetic to the Palestinian's plight. Shame on me for being a
Jew and having empathy for them.

Lastly, it was not until I read Peter Singer and Jim
Mason's, *The Ethics of What We Eat*, did I realize that
becoming a vegan was my answer. "It" finally clicked. I
understood that eating eggs and dairy products was just as
brutal to the animals as eating their flesh. I learned that pain,
sickness, and terror is inherent in these industries. At this
point, I'd already learned about the inhumane suffering of
animals, of the hundreds of miles of dead zone in the Gulf of
Mexico and Chesapeake Bay.

Not because it was the healthy thing to go (and it is) but
because, as a vegan, I am not contributing to the suffering of
another sentient being, a living creature with the consciousness
to experience suffering and pain. As a vegan, I could not only

SAY I was a compassionate person, but live my life compassionately. Not just SAY I care about animals and believe they need not experience a horrid life just for my taste but to live my life lovingly. To "walk the walk".

As a Practical Vegan, I can, on a daily basis, be the woman I imagine I am.

Most religions have their fundamentalist, letter of the law, black and white followers. If you're not with us, you're against us. While that may work for some, it does not work for us.

A Practical Vegan eats no meat. That's NO Meat (chicken/cow/fish/deer, etc). A Practical Vegan consumes no eggs or dairy. That said, above all, a practical vegan adheres, to the best of his/her ability to Donald Watson's original definition: DOES THEIR BEST to be true to the ethos of non-harming of sentient beings.

It is what Zoe Weil, co founder and President of the Institute of Human Education ,calls MOGO, "More Good, Less Harm". For me, to be a practical vegan is to make choices that do just that – create a peaceful, just, compassionate, sustainable world while cultivating my own inner peace and joy.[51].

If you, like my dear friend and co-writer Beth, need to have pharmaceuticals derived from animals – and there is currently no alternative, than you are a practical vegan.

If you wear animal products that were part of your life *prior your journey to veganism*, than you are a practical Vegan.

Feasible, realistic.

---

[51] I highly recommend her book, "*More Good, Less Harm*" and her Institute at humaneeducation.org.

5. SOIL

"Healthy soil leads to healthy plants."
   -Carl Grimm

Soil. Earth. Dirt. We need it to grow our food. You have a seed, plant it in healthy living soil, water it, give it proper sunlight and... voila! The healthier the soil, that is, the more life in it, the more bacteria, microorganisms, and nutrients in the soil, the stronger plants will be. And for the most part, Earth's land is covered with three feet of soil (that is, top soil).

Just about everything we eat requires healthy soil. From the high fructose corn syrup in your soda to the "healthy" farmed fish. Yes, even much of today's farmed fish are fed processed grains and vegetable oils[52] (along with antibiotics, growth hormones, artificial/'natural' coloring).

However, the way in which we use this topsoil, our land, has changed since the first US Farm Bill in 1933. In 1933, there were 6.1 million farms in the United States. Small family farms with an average size of 151 acres. On these acres grew a little over 4 different crops in a rotation. Very healthy for the soil. Some crops take out a particular

---

[52] "Feeding Farmed Fish". Fisheries Committee of the European Parliament,. Federation of European Aquaculture Producers (FEAP) October 2002

nutrient and others put it back in. Jump ahead to 2000. Now, there are 2.1 million farms (about a third) BUT the average size farm is 441 acres. Now, the farm grows one, maybe two crops with no rotation.[53] One crop.

What is different now than in years prior to the 1970s is the way in which we use this topsoil. Not only do we have more people to feed, but we have more livestock to feed. AND, increased number of people being fed are eating cheap meat. For instance, in the developing world, meat consumption rose twice as fast, doubling in the last 20 years. If all the grain currently fed to livestock in the United States were consumed directly by people, the number of people who could be fed would be nearly 800 million," according to David Pimentel, professor of ecology in Cornell University's College of Agriculture and Life Sciences. [54]

However, in recent years, at alarming rates, Earth's earth is vanishing, blowing in the wind, going bu-bye. Poof. According to Professor David Montgomery at Earth and Space Sciences at the University of Washington, we are eroding soil on an order of magnitude that's faster than it's being created -- that is, modern agricultural soil erosion rates are as many as 10 – 100 times faster than soil creation" [55]

DEFORESTATION

In order to 'grow' more meat, animals need to be born, raised, fed, and killed. As the world's appetite for cheap meat increases, (in 1961, world beef production was 71 million tons

---

[53] Carolyn Dimitri, Anne Effland. "Milestones in U.S. Farming and Farm Policy", Amber Waves, June 2005. US Department of Agriculture/Economic Research Service
[54] ttp://www.sciencedaily.com/releases/1997/08/970812003512.htm
[55] http://www.celsias.com/article/dishing-dirt-with-david-montgomery.

but skyrocketed to 284 million tons by 2007)[56] so does it require added land allotted to all phases of the livestock's life. Currently, livestock now uses 30% of the earth's entire land surface[57]

Everywhere in the world, lands are being cleared to make way for crops to feed these animals, buildings to house them and slaughterhouses to kill and 'process' them. (Did I mention the poop that these animals create?)

"Farm animals and animal production facilities cover one-third of the planet's land surface, using more than two-thirds of all available agricultural land including the land used to grow feed crops"[58]

It's not just the people already on this planet, but those to come (world population may reach 7 million in 2012 and 9 million by 2023[59]) and those who will be converting from grain based diet to one more aligned with a Standard American Diet. According to the UN's report, Livestock's Long Shadow, China, human consumption of grain by 7% in rural areas and 45% in urban areas while meat and egg consumption rose by "85% and 278% respectively in rural areas" and 29 and 113% respectively in urban areas". [60]

South America:

Amazon: According to the UN's Livestock's Long Shadow, livestock uses 30% of Earth's land surface. 70% of former forests in the Amazon has been chopped down and pastured. Though agriculture, (up to 35%) logging (3%) and fires (1-2%) are other causes of deforestation in the Amazon, cattle ranching

[56]Mark Bittman, Rethinking-the Meat Guzzler, NY Times. January 27, 2008
[57] FAO Newsroom, "Livestock a major threat to environment" November 29, 2006.
[58] Cees de Haan Henning Steinfeld, Harvey Blackburn.; "Livestock and the environmentt: Finding a Balance" 1997
[59] U.S. Census Bureau, http://www.census.gov/ipc/www/idb/worldpopgraph.php
[60] UN/FAO Report "Livestock's Long Shadow" p. 8, 1:1

by far is the major culprit (65-80%).[61] Brazil is the world's leading exporter of soybeans, [62]in a large part due to the leveling of these ancient forests.

Close to 3,088 square miles of forest were destroyed between August 2007 and August 2008 (a 69% increase over the 1,861 square miles felled in the previous 12 months) according to the National Institute for Space Research, (INPE) which monitors destruction of the Amazon[63].

In Argentina, small local family farms are making way for large CAFOs. One third of the 15,000,000 cattle pass thru feedlots. Up threefold since 2001 [64].

Other areas of deforestation due to grazing:

According to the Farm and Agriculture Organization of the United Nations, "62% of the deforested area in South America will be used for pasture (Central America: 69%), with the pressure particularly strong in Ecuador, Guyana and Venezuela (more than 80%). In Central America, pasture expansion is expected to affect a considerable portion of forest cover in Nicaragua and Panama."

Dr. Neal Barnard, author and president of Physicians Committee for Responsible Medicine, Washington, D.C. says

"About 2,000 pounds of grains must be supplied to livestock in order to produce enough meat and other livestock products to support a person for a year, whereas 400 pounds of grain eaten directly will support a person for a year. Thus, a given quantity

[61] Rhett A. Butler, "Deforestation in the Amazon"
http://www.mongabay.com/brazil.html#cattle
[62] "Meat the Truth"
[63] "Brazil: Amazon Admits Amazon Deforestation on the Rise" Associated Press , August 30, 2008 as sited at http://www.msnbc.msn.com.
[64] Juan Forero, , "Argentine Cattle no longer just home on the Rage", September 14, 2009. Morning Edition, NPR Transcript

of grain eaten directly will feed 5 times as many people as it will if it is eaten indirectly by humans in the form of livestock products." [65]

And although much grain that feeds the livestock is inedible to humans, the point that the resources of the land, the energy that is necessary to feed these animals is wasted on a most inefficient way of obtaining protein is well taken.

A bit of good news:

A growing number of companies are banning goods made by the cattle industry's impact on the Amazon's deforestation. Here's a short list. Regardless of what we think of these companies, we give them "props" for this:

Nike[66]

Timberland [67]

Wal-Mart

Brazil's Top 3 Retailers: CBD, known for its Pao de Acucar supermarkets, and the local subsidiaries of Wal-Mart and Carrefour SA.[68]

---

[65] http://www.gaia.com /quotes/neal_barnard#ixzz0T19StUn

[66] http://www.greenpeace.org/usa/news/nike-establishes-policy-072209

[67] Timberlane's blog: http://www.earthkeeper.com/blog/?s=deforestation

[68]"Brazil Retailers Ban Beef from cleared Amazon Area". Reuters, June 12, 2009

6. VEGAN HEALTH

Do you picture a vegan as someone who is way too skinny, pale and sickly? Nothing is further from the truth! (Do Pamela Anderson or Carl Lewis look like they are unwell?) A vegetarian diet is supportive to your health in many ways. For instance, there are at least 3 dozen plants that have been identified as plants that help protect us from cancer. Among those are broccoli, cauliflower, berries and many nuts. [69]

In one study, lifelong vegetarians had a 24 percent lower incidence and lifelong vegans (those who eat no eggs or dairy products) had a 57 percent lower incidence of coronary heart disease compared to meat eaters [70]. Healthy volunteers who consumed a vegetarian diet (25% of calories as fat) that was rich in green, leafy vegetables and other low-calorie vegetables (tomatoes, cucumbers, carrots, bell peppers, celery, green beans, etc.), fruits, nuts, sweet corn and peas experienced after two weeks decreases of 25, 33, 20 and 21 percent in total cholesterol, LDL cholesterol, triglycerides, and total/HDL cholesterol ratio, respectively (15). [71]

---

[69]Craig WJ. Nutrition and Wellness. A Vegetarian Way to Better Health. Golden Harvest Books, Berrien Springs, MI, 1999
[70] Thorogood M, Carter R, et al. Plasma lipids and lipoprotein cholesterol concentrations in people with different diets in Britain. *Br Med J* 1987;295: 351-3.
[71]Jenkins DJA, Popovich D, Kendall C, et al. Effect of a diet high in vegetables, fruit, and nuts on serum lipids. *Metabolism* 1997;46:530-7

The debate about soy or soya products: some studies and organizations have made some significant claims against soy products stating that soy foods are harmful to one's health. However, according to John Robbins, author of *Diet For a New America,* and *Food Revolution,* in his article *"What about Soy?":*

"It's true that soybeans contain substances that in excess (emphasis is ours) can be harmful. But to imply, as some do, that as a result eating soyfoods poses a risk to human health is taking things much further than the evidence warrants. There would be dangers in eating a diet based entirely on soybeans. But, then, the same could be said for broccoli or any other healthy food. This is one of the reasons why varied diets are so important. Diversity protects. For most people under most circumstances, soy products are a healthful addition to a balanced diet that includes plenty of vegetables, whole grains, seeds, nuts, fruits, and other legumes. For most people, substituting soyfoods for some of the animal foods they now eat is one of the healthiest dietary changes they could make."

Another issue with soy to note is its contribution to the world's deforestation as well as the use of fertilizers and pesticides. Over 85% of the close to 230 billion metric tons of soybeans are crushed into soybean meal for livestock feed or for vegetable oil[72]. Approximately 10% of soybeans are used directly as human food for tofu, soymilk, soy dairy products, (95%in Asia)[73] and another 4-5% is processed into soy protein and flours (for dairy/meat alternatives, infant formulas, nutritional supplements in food, energy bars.)[74] while the remaining soy is processed into meal for animal feed. .

Veganism and vegetarianism gives a plethora of healthy and delicious choices. One can easily be a junk -food vegan,

---

[72] Mian N. Riaz. "Soy Application In Food", p. 12 CRC Press 2006
[73] http://www.soyatech.com/soy_facts.htm
[74] Mian N. Riaz. "Soy Application In Food", p. 12 CRC Press 2006

just like you can be a junk food meat eater. There are vegan s'mores, vegan cookies, potato chips, French fries (unless fried in beef fat)....well, you get the picture. (See Chapter 11 for some recipes for tasty treats) The more we eat food in its natural state, the healthier it is.

Here's an example of a vegan food pyramid[75].

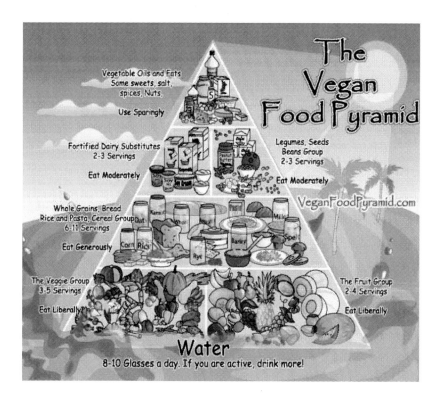

The food choices within veganism are vast, and growing daily. If you think about it, you will find that it is the vegetarian food that makes non vegetarian food interesting. How would a hamburger be without the bun, lettuce and tomato? Most fries are vegetarian. (if not fried in beef tallow, of course) How about a BBQ dinner without slaw and potato salad or chips? W.H. Kellogg, pioneer in the process of making flaked cereal – yeah – those Kelloggs, and a vegetarian once said that a vegetarian is someone who just eats side dishes[76] Vegetarian food makes life interesting.

Vegan Outreach writes, *"Well-planned vegan [pure vegetarian] and other types of vegetarian diets are appropriate for all stages of the life cycle, including during pregnancy, lactation, infancy, childhood, and adolescence. Vegetarian diets offer a number of nutritional benefits, including lower levels of saturated fat, cholesterol, and animal protein as well as higher levels of carbohydrates, fiber, magnesium, potassium, folate, and antioxidants such as vitamins C and E and phytochemicals. Vegetarians have been reported to have lower body mass indices than non vegetarians, as well as lower rates of death from ischemic heart disease; vegetarians also show lower blood cholesterol levels; lower blood pressure; and lower rates of hypertension, type 2 diabetes, and prostate and colon cancer."* [77]

Being vegan can improve your health, your energy and your quality of life!

---

[76] http://www.squidoo.com/vegetarian-quotes
[77] http://www.veganoutreach.org/whyvegan/health.html

"Right now" Resources for further reading

Choose Veg
http://www.chooseveg.com/vegan-health.asp

Vegan Health
http://www.veganhealth.org

Vegan Outreach
http://www.veganoutreach.org/whyvegan/health.html

7.   STEREOTYPES and POLICE

When you picture a vegan, many stereotypes may come into your mind – a long haired odoriferous hippy, a young angry person covered with tattoos and upset with society or maybe just a wimpy string-bean of a person.

While these people certainly exist, they are not the vegan norm. Vegans come in all shapes, sizes, colors and ages. Some people go vegan at a young age like six or seven. Some don't go vegan until they are past their fifties or sixties.

Carl Lewis, a vegan, won nine Olympic gold medals. There are vegan body builders. Vegan middle aged moms (like us) that are neither built like a toothpick or are tattooed.

Vegans from the world of entertainment include Casey Affleck, Pamela Anderson, Ed Begley Jr., Linda Blair, and James Cromwell.

Musicians include Bryan Adams, Paul McCartney, Moby, Morrissey, Robin Gibb and Lenny Kravitz. There are vegans in all areas politics (like Dennis Kucinich) and athletics (NBA basketball player John Salley). This list is in no way representative of all the vegans out there. This is a small list to let you know that vegans vary as widely as veggies!

"Right now" Resources for further reading

Global Onesess
http://www.experiencefestival.com/list_of_vegans

Wikipedia
http://en.wikipedia.org/wiki/List_of_vegans

Happy Cow
http://www.happycow.net/famous_vegetarians.html

Vegan Police

We are not the Vegan Police. You can be certain, as you follow this path and make choices that exclude animals products, you will encounter them. Perhaps on-line, perhaps in your "real life". Either way, they are there.

Just what are the Vegan Police? Well, unlike actual police officers, they are not here to help you in your moments of need, or even inquiry. Instead, they ridicule and condemn others for a cadre of 'infractions', from consuming products with refined sugar – vegan or otherwise, to insisting that you are not a "REAL" vegan if you (fill in the blank) or, you don't count as a vegan if choose to exclude animal products from your diet and or life due to environmental reasons. We happen to think that the cow, chicken, duck, cat doesn't care WHY you don't eat them.

The Vegan Police, (we'll give them the benefit of the doubt here) are well meaning but, unlike *Practical* Vegans, do not look at the big picture – that by eliminating these products animals lives WILL be saved...be it 10, 50, 100 or more in a year.

Furthermore, many in the Armed Forces of Veganism may not fully understand that by-products of animals permeate our society.

Hidden animal by-products

Animal by-products are everywhere – even in places you may not expect...here's a brief list:

Carmine/Carminic Acid: crushed up bugs. Yes, ground up dried insects called cochineals: used as red food coloring often found in 'fruit' drinks, juices, cosmetics, popsicles and yogurt. Note that, in January 2009, the US Food and Drug Administration passed a new regulation.[78]requiring carmine and cochineal to be listed by name on the label. This regulation is effective January 5, 2011.

Glycerides (mono-, di-, and triglycerides): Though glycerol from animal fats or plants, (labels do not always list its derivative): Processed foods, cosmetics, perfumes, lotions, inks, glues, automobile antifreeze. Used as emulsifier

Lactic acid: Acid formed by bacteria acting on the milk sugar lactose. Creates a tart flavor.: Cheese, yogurt, pickles, olives, sauerkraut, candy, frozen desserts, chewing gum, fruit preserves, dyeing and textile printing

Lecithin: Coloring from egg yolks. May also be derived from soybeans *(Labels do not always list its derivative):*

Pancreatin (pancreatic extract): Cows or hogs: Digestive aids/some contact lens solutions

---

[78] http://www.foodnavigator-usa.com/Product-Categories/Flavors-and-colors/New-labeling-rules-for-cochineal-bug-coloring

Stearic Acid: Tallow, other animal fats (usually from the stomach of pigs[79]) and oils: lubricant, in soaps, cosmetics, food packaging, deodorant sticks, toothpastes, and as a softener in rubber

While we support the rights of the passionate, often fanatical vegans to do what they do (legally, that is) in the name of health, animals and our planet we believe it is more important to encourage and even persuade you to take action(s) to becoming a Practical Vegan.

---

[79] http://www.happycow.net/health-animal-ingredients.html

8. WATER

"In the last few decades entire new categories of waste have come to plague and menace the American scene. These are the technological wastes--the by-products of growth, industry, agriculture, and science. We cannot wait for slow evolution over generations to deal with them..."

-Lyndon B. Johnson, *Special Message to the Congress on Conservation and Restoration of Natural Beauty*, February 8, 1965

      Lagoon. La-gooon. Ahhhh. When you read the word 'lagoon' what image comes to mind? A beautiful tropical scene? Serene and magical. Delicate aromas wafting leisurely in your nose. A waterfall cascading into a secluded cool pool of pristine blue water? Well, as you may have guessed, the lagoons in this chapter are, well, not those lagoons. Instead they are repulsive concrete pits and reservoirs, which hold between to 20 to 45 million gallons of manure and urine. (A properly sized lagoon includes 10,000 gallons of storage per year per cow[80] and 190 gallons per pig during its stay on a

---

[80] Chuzhao Lin, "Bring Your Lagoon Back to Life", http://www.proactmicrobial.com/images/Hoards%20article.pdf.

farm[81]) Oh – and the largest feedlot? Grand View (yeah, I'll bet) in Illinois. It boasts a feed lot of 750 acres, the largest holding capacity and a "one-time capacity of 150,000 head." [82]

Getting back to that "load of crap", picture this: You poop. How much do YOU, um, make in, say, a day, a week, a year. (The *average person* poops 100-400 grams a day[83] - or 80-321 pounds per year, barring any illness). Now think of a cow. An average Holstein cow produces about 65 pounds of poop and 3.5 gallons of pee – **a DAY**[84]. Each day – each cow – 65 lbs of poo = 23,725 pound a year. That's ONE COW!

So, when you, ehem, relieve yourself, you sit, go, wipe, and flush. Your eliminations are pumped to a treatment facility and, through a series of highly monitored steps, including screening, grit removal, more filtration, biological nutrient removal and disinfection,[85] is released back into the water supply.

However, elimination(s) of CAFO (concentrated animal feeding operation) animals is untreated. Nothing filtered, screened or removed. Lest you think "but it's just poop – it comes from nature" – not so fast. Yes there are plant nutrients such as nitrogen and phosphorus but also

- antibiotic-resistant bacteria
- hormones
- chemicals used in livestock care
- milkhouse wastes
- cleaning agents
- ammonia and heavy metals

[81] John D. Lawrence, Returns from Finishing Feeder Pigs, (File B133, August 2008), http://www.extension.iastate.edu/agdm/livestock/html/b1-33.html.
[82] www.simplot.com
[83] Marianne Strasse-Wolthuis, Martijn B. Katan, Joseph G.A.J. Hautvast. American Journal of Clinical Nutrition, Letter to The Editor via www.afcn.org
[84] http://www.fergusonfoundation.org/hbf cow_in_out/cowmoreinfo.html.
[85] http://www.lasvegasnevada.gov/files/BRO-WPCF_04.pdf

- *silage leachate. [86] (*high-moisture fodder that can be stored and fed to ruminants (cud-chewing animals like cattle and sheep). Silage leachate forms when water is allowed into the silage and it washes through the decomposing materials. If the leachate is not contained, it can get into water, bringing with it enormous amounts of nutrients, causing algae blooms, and decreases in dissolved oxygen (Source: Glossary of CAFO terms, Michigan Sierra Club Website)

The waste is stored in those lovely open lagoons where, seepage and overflow is inevitable. And, at any time in the process, there can be leaks or breaks. These nasty cesspools can be as large as seven acres and hold 20 to 45 MILLION GALLONS of "waste" water. Most factory farms store animal waste in open lagoons as large as several football fields. Lagoons routinely burst, sending millions of gallons of manure into waterways and spreading microbes that can cause gastroenteritis, fevers, kidney failure, and death"[87] And where does it go? Into the earth, finding its way to our rivers, then our bays and finally, the open ocean. Imagine, chicken poop – in the open ocean.

Down by The Bay

One of the hardest hit areas being polluted more and more is the beautiful Chesapeake Bay. The largest estuary in the United States, the Chesapeake is surrounded by Virginia and Maryland. Rivers, streams, and ground water travel from New York, Pennsylvania, Delaware, Maryland, Virginia, and West Virginia [88] and emptying in the bay. Pollution anywhere along the way makes its way to the bay. The pollution has all

---

[86]http://michigan.sierraclub.org/issues/greatlakes/articles/cafofacts.html.waste
[87] "Cesspool of Shame", National Defense Council, Clean Water Network, July 2001.
[88] Fact Sheet 102-98 - The Chesapeake Bay: Geologic Product of Rising Sea Level". U. S. Geological Survey. 1998-11-18

but wiped out the precious oyster beds and threatens other wildlife and marine life. The crab population alone has dropped 70% since the 1980s.[89]

The biggest culprit? Poop. Well, not JUST poop, as you've already learned. And not just any poop. Untreated poultry poop. In 1960, in Maryland, there were 90 million chickens that produced 126 tons of manure. At that rate, small farms were able to "reuse" the poop. The nitrogen in the waste is ideal for growing many crops. (talk about recycling). [90]

However, in 2008, the state's chicken farms, most of which are no longer the quaint small family farms, squeezed out 1.2 BILLION pounds of...of...well, ya know. However, unlike its 1960 predecessor, this waste product isn't just sweet smelling poop. Nope. Like the Iowa's hog poop, this stuff contains a lot more. And all that "a lot more" ends up, you guessed it, in the Bay.

When too many nutrients like nitrogen or phosphorous from agricultural runoff, fertilizers from croplands, and other sources empty in the Bay, they fuel algae blooms. (Even more unwanted nutrients drop into all bodies around the world via raindrops and other atmospheric processes. Robert Diaz, professor at Virginia Institute of Marine Science at the College of William and Mary says that 1/4 of the nitrogen affecting coastal areas comes from the atmosphere.[91]) When there are more algae than Bay's predators can consume, the extra nutrients sink to the bay's bottom.

---

[89] Ian Urbina, "On Maryland, Focus on Poultry Industry Pollution" New York Times, November 28, 2008
[90] ibid
[91] 'Dead Zones' Expand in Coastal Waters Around the World, Science In The News". September 8, 2008 Voice Of America Interview Transcript

There they decompose in a process that depletes water of oxygen needed by other organisms. [92] No oxygen means no life. Hypoxia. No life is a dead zone. Dead.

The Chesapeake Bay dead zone, 282 cubic billion feet[93], loses close to 5% of the Bay's total production of food energy[94] is sadly, not the only dead zone on the planet. It is estimated that there are over 400 dead zones in the world, covering close to 95,000 square miles of sea[95], primarily in the Northern Hemisphere along coastal waters.

Other Dead Zones include:
- Reoccurring (seasonal) dead zone along Oregon's coast as well as off the coast of San Diego, California and Lake Erie,
- The Gulf of Mexico: 22,126 sq kilometers (8,543 sq miles),
- Baltic Sea: The World's largest dead zone: about 38,000 square miles[96], roughly the size of Estonia[97]: Has lost about 30% of its available food energy[98]
- Seto Island Sea: Japan: semi enclosed basin

Usage

How much water does an average person? According to The American Water Works Association, a single family uses

---

[92] Karl Blankenship. "Large Spring Algae blooms pose array of possibilities" Bay Journal. June 1996

[93] Dr. Bill Chameides, "Predicting Dead Zones"The Green Grok, Nicholas Insider, July 2009,

[94] David Malmquist, "Dead Zones Continue to Spread". August 14, 2008. http://www.vims.edu/newsandevents/topstories/2008-dead-zones-spread.php.

[95] David Perlman. "Scientists Alarmed by Ocean Dead-Zone Growth". San Francisco Chronicle, .August 15, 2008.

[96] http://www.ehponline.org/docs/2000/108-3/focus.html

[97] Fran Weaver, "Baltic Dead Zone Spreading" Helsinki Times, General News, September 1, 2008

[98] http://www.commondreams.org/archive/2008/08/15/11004

45-70 gallons of water per day (depending on efficiency of water fixtures)

How water much does an average cow use annually?) Well, according to the United States Geological Society, each cow drinks 30-45 gallons of water a day[99]

According to David Pimentel, PhD, Professor Emeritus of Ecology and Evolutionary Biology at Cornell University and author of *Food, Energy, and Society*, the U.S. agriculture accounts for 87% of all the fresh water consumed each year. Livestock directly use only 1.3% of that water. But when the water required for forage and grain production is included, livestock's water usage rises dramatically. Every kilogram of beef produced takes 100,000 liters of water. Some 900 liters of water go into producing a kilogram of wheat. Potatoes are even less "thirsty," at 500 liters per kilogram.[100]

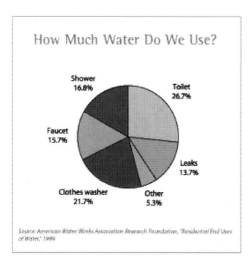

You live on the Delmarva (DELaware / MARyland/VirginA) Peninsula, the 6,057 square miles of land that separate the Chesapeake Bay from the Atlantic Ocean.

---

[99] *http://ga.water.usgs.gov/edu/wulv.html*
[100] http://www.news.cornell.edu/releases/aug97/livestock.hrs.html

You love farming but more and more, it's bringing in less money. Other farms have more chickens. You need a lot of space to let your chickens roam or at least walk around a little. (Though you don't want them going all cardio on you and losing weight. After all, this is no spa.)

Your neighbor just bought into a contract from the big chicken producing company. He'll need to lay out the cash for building the enormous shed that will house the 25,000 – 30,000 birds. He'll feed the birds the cheap corn and soy that The Company will provide (which works out just great because three quarters of Maryland's crops go to feeding poultry). Then he'll be responsible for heating and cooling the sheds. Oh, and any changes the company demands...er..um..requires...will come out of his bank account.

In return, your buddy will get the poultry, the actual (eggs or chickens??). After the chickens (now given names based on their cooking status: broiler, fryer, roaster) have plumped up to an unhealthy 40+ pounds in 42 days[101], they will be slaughtered and packaged and sold under the name of that major international company. No credit given to the actual farmer. And, as chicken becomes a cheaper "food product", guess who gets choked? The Big Company? No.

The Company owns the product. It does not own the product of the product, namely, the waste. Below is an excerpt of an interview with Mr. Jim Perdue, Chairman of Perdue Farms, Inc. from PBS's Frontline, "Poisoned Water"

FRONTLINE: Help me understand one thing that's also got me baffled. ... How do you wind up owning the chickens, owning the feed and not owning, in the sense of legal responsibility, the manure?

---

[101] "Poultry Growers Rattled" Anita Huslin. The Washington Post, July 7, 2003, pB1

MR. PERDUE: The manure is considered a resource, actually. You know, when we went to Kentucky, they're used to buying chemical fertilizer to fertilize their hay. They think they've died and gone to heaven now because they've got a fertilizer that's organic also, which chemical [fertilizer] is not, so to them it's a big benefit. ... It's not a matter of who owns or doesn't own it; it's a matter of what use is being made from it.

Ha. That's funny. And the United States' governmental organization responsible for said pollution, the EPA issued rules that create another huge loophole for these industrialized operations to claim that they don't discharge into waterways and so don't need to be regulated - at all. It sounds ludicrous, but, in fact, it's true. NRDC, the Waterkeeper Alliance, and the Sierra Club have challenged this rule, but EPA has not yet agreed to revise it. The first step in cleaning up this mess is to require factory farms to come into the regulatory system. Congress asked EPA to do that in 1972. [102] The Bay is still waiting for the EPA to comply.

[102]Nancy Stoner, "Poisoned Waters", April 20, 2009.
http://switchboard.nrdc.org/blogs/nstoner/poisoned_waters.html

9. BUSTING VEGAN FEARS

When embarking on any new experience there may be certain accompanying anxieties/worries. Here are a few common "what if" questions you may encounter on your vegan path:

What if I...

Q. What if I start and fail? I'll be embarrassed. I'll feel like a failure...

A. What if you don't fail? You will deprive yourself, the animals and the environment of the benefits of your going vegan because of something that may not happen. Most of us don't let potential risks stop us from driving and going where we want to go. Don't let a fear or insecurity stop you from living the life you want to live or from being who you want to be.

Q: What if I decide this isn't for me and then eat meat 6 months down the road? If I've broadcasted to everyone I know but then have a burger or a chicken nugget, I'll be embarrassed or feel like a failure.

A. What if you try it and it still <u>is</u> for you six months down the road? And, even if it isn't, you have taken time and cleaned out your body. You will be healthier six months down the road, and statistically, your six months of being vegan would have saved the lives of about 50 animals! That isn't a failure at all!

There are also fears of the future and social situations:

Q. I can't eat at a restaurant anymore. What will I do when my friends go out to eat or I want a quick bite?

A. You can still eat almost anywhere, and more than salad too! Just like at home, where almost any recipe can be "veganised", as can restaurant meals. Ask if the chef can toss the pasta with olive oil and garlic instead of cream sauce for instance. Check out their menu online or call ahead. Often, the host or even the chef will accommodate you, just as if you had an allergy to, say, dairy. Pre-planning will prove fruitful and may provide you with useful information about the restaurant and it's choices. The world is still open to you!

Q. I can't eat in social environments anymore. I'll miss a lot of outings!

A. Sure you can. We do it all the time! It is helpful to bring your own dish to socials, and who knows – they may be so good that you inspire others to go vegan with you. We can testify – there is nothing like a vegan friend! Maybe talk to the host, explain, inquire. Your hosts concern should be that you have a good time and, if he/she is like our mothers, that you don't walk away from the table hungry.

Q . I can't go vegan because of all the non-vegan things I have in my closet I can't afford to replace. If I can't go all the way right away then I guess I can't go vegan!

A. This is <u>practical veganism</u>. People choose to handle this in a variety of ways. There are a few who can afford to immediately rid themselves of non-vegan clothing, shoes, coats and other items and replace them with vegan ones, that is not the case for most of us.

Many will give away non-vegan items that are not needed, and then wear out the articles they already own. There are very "vegan" aspects to this too. You are being thrifty, not creating more waste, and you are honoring both yourself and the animal. Yourself – because you are still honoring the person you were – the choices you made before you went vegan. You are honoring the animal by making sure that every little bit of its life left in your care went to good use.

Q. People will think I am a hypocrite if I say I'm vegan while wearing non-vegan clothing I got before I turned vegan

A. Yes, you may indeed run into "vegan police" - but if you do, just politely inform them that these are things you got before you were vegan. If it bothers them, you could always ask them if they would like to replace the item for you. There are lots of on line vegan shops in our resource section at the end of this book!

10. MORE STRAIGHT TALK

Pull up a chair, pour yourself a cup of your favorite coffee, and let's chat a minute. Whether you decide to go 100% vegan, vegetarian, vegan two days a week, or just give up red meat – know that what you do makes a difference. It makes a difference to your health, to our environment and to the animals.

It doesn't have to be all or nothing. Every little thing makes a difference.

We wrote this book to show you that you can make a difference, and you don't have to fit in a box someone else drew. Life is a journey. Veganism is a journey. Enjoy it. Embrace the changes as you grow. You may start out simply cutting out chicken from your diet and end up a vegetarian years later. Even if you try going vegan for six months and you go back to your old way of eating, there was still an impact – both to your health and to the world. It doesn't have to be all or nothing.

Brands

If you try a new food and don't like it – it may be the brand. Try another one. Sounds obvious. Doesn't it? It really makes a difference in vegan foods though. There are some brands of soy milk we adore, and some brands we can barely swallow. There are some that Susan loves but Beth could just "pass" on. Same with tofu, tempeh, vegan cheeses etc. Don't conclude you don't like a food after trying only one brand. Give a few a shot. You might be surprised!

Friendships

Finding people that support your new lifestyle is important. Hook up with some local vegans. There are vegan meet-ups in many places around the world. You can also find other vegans online. Even non-vegan friends that are willing to explore new vegan foods and restaurants with you is fabulous. Hooray for them and now you two have something more in common!

Cookbooks

We've given you some recipes to get started, but we would each like to recommend our three favorite Vegan Cookbooks to you. Great cookbooks with easy, reliable recipes makes getting started so much easier!

Beth's

1. How it all Vegan by Sarah Kramer: all around great "vegan bible". Recipes we grew up with veganized. Most can be made under 30 minutes. She also includes

a large section on easy, cheap ways to make your own vegan cleaning products and other household items.

2. <u>Vegan-A-Go-Go</u> by Sarah Kramer: Around 150 easy quick recipes that will impress – you and others! Awesome Alfredo Sauce and chocolate chip cookies....LOVE this pint size cookbook

3. <u>PETA's Vegan Collage Cookbook:</u> All these recipes are made in the microwave. Very quick. Uses many prepared ingredients. Great for weekends or long days where you just don't want to cook but have to eat – and want something that tastes good. Think of it as a McDonald's {{cringe}} substitute.

Susan's

1. <u>Vegan Planet</u> by Robin Robertson: Interesting and tasty recipes from all over the world

2. <u>Eat, Drink and Be Vegan</u> by Dreena Burton...very helpful recipes when hosting or when you needs to bring a goodie to a pot-luck

3. <u>Vegan Cupcakes take over The World</u> by Isa Chandra Moskowitz, Terry Hope Romero and Sara Quin...easy to understand recipes. So delicious that the most finicky carnivore would be pleased

11. LAST WORDS

Disconnect, the contradiction between saying one loves animals and eating them, hunting them, wearing them. This disconnect is rampant in our culture. Humans are amazing. We are able to rationalize *anything*. (Kudos to the meat and dairy lobby for this).

With about 74.8 million dogs and 88.3 million cats owned in the US[103], we love our pets. Americans spend, on average, 41 billion dollars on them. [104] Every state in the United States and the District of Columbia has laws prohibiting cruelty to animals with a fine and or jail time for the convicted.

Yet, people eat other animals. Beliefs that animals are "so stupid" (e.g. turkeys who, it is incorrectly thought, are so stupid that they will look up in the rain and drown[105]) or "cannot feel anyhow" makes it seemingly easier for people to disassociate "love" for animals with their paradoxical consumption of them. Meat-eaters allow them to be tortured, to exist in horrendous, repulsive environs. They condone this behavior by purchasing the animals' flesh, parts and fluids and eggs as "products" because they believe it to be their birthright as Humans.

---

[103]"U.S. Pet Ownership Statistics" American Pet Products Manufacturers Association (APPMA) 2007-2008 National Pet Owners Survey
[104] Diane Brady and Christopher Palmeri . "The Pet Economy". Business Week. August 6, 2007
[105] http://www.snopes.com/critters/wild/turkey.asp

We understand this dichotomy exists. We too have and continue to confront the "we need some animal protein" and "it's okay, I just eat free range, grass fed, organic, cage free, no antibiotic, humane eggs/milk/meat." We hope you will examine your own thoughts about this.

It was also our intention to revel to you the ills of a meat based lifestyle (not just diet) for our planet. It is, after all, "the only one we've got". To leave a legacy of pollution to our children and their children, solely for our taste buds is, at the very least selfish and inhumane.

Whether you come to veganism for non-violence, abolitionist, health, or environmental reasons will make no difference to the animal. It will make a difference in your life and the life of our planet.

12: RECIPES

Getting Started

Think you can't be a vegan because you live with meat eaters? Maybe you are actually responsible for cooking for them. Think to be a vegetarian you have to make two meals each night and spend all day in the kitchen? After reading this, you will change your mind. The goal of this chapter is to show you how prepare luscious meals to fulfill your vegetarian needs *as well as make useful suggestions for complimentary side dishes your meat eating family requests.*

We understand this is unusual. First, it is *very unusual* for a book touting veganism in any way to provide suggestions for including meat. This will, no doubt confuse and anger some very passionate people.

And yet, we also understand that some vegetarians do not have the "luxury" of making only vegan meals for their family. In our homes, we have meat eaters. We lead by example and, though we are the primary shoppers and cooks, we do not force our loved ones to make the same choices we do. Instead, we see this as opportunity for us to a)lead by example and b) shows our love and respect for the humans in our lives by not condemning them for the lifestyle – culinary or otherwise – that they make. (and no, in our eyes, this is not akin to living with murderers, rapists, torturers, or pedophiles)

68

Another unusual tidbit; these recipes include no salads - green salads, bean salads, or any. We believe you've "been around the block" and have already had your share. We are confident you know how to put together a yummy salad!

This chapter is "matter-of-fact,". short and succinct. It includes useful entrees and desserts we hope you will implement as a starting (or continuing) point for your vegan lifestyle.

Why?

We are assuming you are reading the recipes because either: you

▶ are a vegan with meat eaters in your household
▶ like vegetarian and vegan foods on occasion but live with people that "need meat" at every meal or
▶ are interested in vegan cooking and need some solid recipes to start.
▶ cooking for a vegetarian or vegan in the family.

The following recipes keep to our K.I.S.S. philosophy. "Keep It Simple Sweetie." We hope to help make your life easier. First, by letting you know that moving toward and becoming vegan need not be a harrowing, "pull out your hair", "what am I gonna eat" process. Second, by providing you with these tools and helping you along your way.

There are almost a month's worth of main dishes here. Even if you never bought another cookbook, you can still make a different dinner almost every night of the week each month, month in month-out.

Most people make the same 10-12 meals week in-week out with a few extras thrown in here and there. Our goal is to supply you with some basic recipes that do not rely on expensive meat substitutes or vegan "fast foods". These recipes are simple, healthy, delicious and cost effective that can fulfill your needs for your core meals – a vegan "bible" if you will, for blended families.

Once your family tries these recipes, they may decide to "go vegan" too. Each entrée will have a suggestion for integrating meat into a portion of the vegetarian dish or an easy "meaty" side dish for the meat lovers of the household.

We encourage you to play with these recipes, make them your own. Be creative.

Bon Appétit!

Buon Appetito!

¡Buen provecho!

Enjoy!

The Practical Side of Cooking:

There are four basic patterns for combining vegetarian and meat-lovers meals.

1) *The side dish:* Use the vegetarian main course as the meat eater's side dish.

2) *One sauce, Two Bases*: Have a common vegetarian sauce or spread that can be used over two different bases – one meat, one vegetable or grain. A lentil sauce, for example, can be eaten over rice, or ground beef. This will satisfy the needs of the vegetarian and the meat eater with one simple sauce.

3) *Divide and conquer*: Make one vegetarian meal, separating out the meat eater's portion about ¾ of the way through the cooking process, and adding meat to their portion

4) *Two Sauces, One Base*: Make two different sauces (one veggie, one meat) and have the same base – for example a marinara sauce and a meat sauce would both go over the same base: spaghetti noodles.

Whenever possible, there will be suggestions how to incorporate meat with a portion of the vegetarian entree so you have cooked ONE meal satisfying the meat lovers and the vegetarians.

This book will <u>not</u>, however, provide the meaty recipes. If for instance, meatloaf is suggested as a meat portion and you don't have your own meatloaf recipe. *The meat dishes suggested choose meat recipes that tend to be simple to make with minimal preparation time.*

*Another time saver if you *must fix meat* for a family member: make the weeks' worth of meat all at one time (saves money too as you can buy in bulk). In glass jars with secure lids, store the cooked meat you will use later.

Breakfast

French Toast

Voilà. Tres bon! This is scrumptious. Oui, Oui!

1 ½ cups soy milk

2 1/2 Tablespoons unbleached flour

1 packet of Sweet and Low (or use raw/organic sugar)

1 ½ teaspoons ground cinnamon

1 ½ Tablespoons vegetable oil

4-6 slices of stale wheat bread

Mix "milk", flour, cinnamon and sweet and low in a blender until smooth. Pour mixture into shallow bowl or casserole dish. Spray oil in a non-stick fry pan. Dip bread into mixture, coating both sides and place in skillet. Fry each side over Medium to Medium-High until golden brown and crispy – about 3 minutes a side. Remove from pan and keep warm in oven while remaining slices cook.

Serve with Karo corn syrup or maple syrup.

Pancakes

There's nothing like pancakes and a hot cup of coffee to start the morning off right!

1 cup flour

2 Tablespoons sugar

2 Teaspoons baking powder

1/8 teaspoon salt

½ to 2/3 cup soy milk

3 Tablespoons vegetable oil + additional oil for frying

Combine the flour, sugar, salt and baking powder in a bowl. Mix well. Pour in soy milk and oil.

Beat until smooth.

Measure 1/3 cup of batter onto hot oiled griddle. When bubbles appear, flip pancake over with a spatula. Cook pancake another 2 minutes. Remove from pan and keep warm in the over while the rest of pancakes bake.

Sugar Free Chocolate Smoothie

Chocolate – what a luscious way to start the day!!

2 cups plain soy milk or rice milk

1 teaspoon vanilla

1-2 frozen bananas – chopped before blending

3 Tablespoons cocoa powder

1 Tablespoon liquid sweetener

Combine all in blender. Mix until smooth. Pour into glasses and enjoy!

Scrambled Tofu

I To-fu, do you To-fu?

1 package firm tofu – drained and crumbled

1 medium onion – chopped

1 teaspoon curry powder

½ teaspoon garlic powder

¼ cup chopped mushrooms

3 Tablespoons vegetable oil for frying

salt and pepper to taste

In large frying pan, sauté onions and mushrooms over medium-high heat until onions are translucent. Crumble tofu into pan, add curry powder and garlic powder. Fry an additional 10minutes, or until all moisture from tofu has evaporated. Serves 2, or 1 with leftovers: mix with egg-less mayonnaise for a vegan egg salad sandwich.

Other Breakfast Suggestions:

Hot or Cold Cereal with fruit

Peanut Butter and honey sandwiches

"Buttered" toast or bagels

Bagels with vegan cream cheese

Leftovers

Miso Soup

Nuts and dried fruit mix

Main Dishes

Nutty Lentil Loaf

Better than meat loaf ever dreamed of being. Here's something for the nut in all of us! Sometimes you feel like a nut. Sometimes you don't.

1 cup of thickly stewed lentils – drain liquid and reserve

1 Tablespoon onion powder

1 Tablespoon garlic powder

1 Tablespoon dried cilantro

½ cup finely chopped nuts of your choice

¼ cup ketchup

½ cup bread crumbs

½ cup shredded rice mozzarella grated cheese

Mix all the ingredients and place in a bowl. If too dry, add reserved lentil liquid 1 Tablespoon at a time. Mixture should be dense and hefty. Shape into meat loaf pan sprayed with cooking oil, and bake at 375 for 25 minutes or until a toothpick placed in the center comes out clean. Top with either ketchup or brown gravy. Serve with mashed potatoes or sweet potato fries and a salad. Serves: 4

For the Meat Eater: A sandwich would make a nice compliment to this meal. Or, you could always make a meatloaf side by side with the nut loaf. Just know that yours will taste better.

Lo-Mein

Lo-Mein in Spain falls mainly on the plain. Well, maybe not, We get confused. This dish however, is not confusing but is quite tasty!

6 oz of cooked linguine

1 t sesame oil

3 Tablespoons Olive oil

4 oz. Extra firm tofu – cubed (*Freeze the tofu for 24 hours and then defrost for a heartier texture)

1 small carrot – thinly sliced

¼ cup green peas

½ zucchini, finely chopped

¼ teaspoons ginger powder

1 garlic clove – minced

1 ½ Tablespoons soy sauce

2 green onions – chopped

Toss cooked linguine with sesame oil and set aside. Warm 1 tablespoon olive oil in a medium skillet over medium heat. Add tofu and fry until golden brown on all sides. Toss tofu with the noodles. Reheat skillet over medium high heat and using remaining 2 tablespoons of oil, sauté garlic for 5 minutes, until tender. Add remaining vegetables and stir fry until veggies are tender.

Add remaining ½ teaspoon of soy sauce and stir fry noodle mixture with veggies. Serve immediately. Goes well with salad.

For the Meat Eater: Toss in a portion of cooked seafood, and serve with an all vegetable salad or serve, as is, with a hearty Chef Salad.

Portobello Steaks

Mouth watering and hearty. A yummy, healthy, good for your heart alternative to a steak.

2 whole Portobello mushrooms –stems removed

¼ cup olive oil

2 cloves of garlic – peeled and finely minced

1 Tablespoon Tamari

2 teaspoons vegan steak sauce

1 teaspoon sugar

Put Portobello mushrooms in a zip lock bag or bowl. Mix olive oil, garlic, sauces and sugar and pour over Portobello's in bag. Let marinate in the refrigerator at least one hour. The longer, the better.

Place marinated mushrooms into a baking pan, bottom side up. Put under broiler and broil until browned. Turn over. Brown other side. Serve with pan juices poured over the top.

Great with potatoes and garlic bread.

For the Meat Eater: On a separate broiling pan, broil a steak at the same time you broil the mushrooms.

Spaghetti Sauce

Spaghetti is a classic. Maybe this will be your new classic sauce.

1 small onion – chopped

1 Tablespoon olive oil

1 small carrot – chopped

3 garlic cloves – minced

1 – 14 oz can of tomato sauce

2 teaspoons dried basil

1 teaspoon salt

¼ cup fresh parsley – minced

1 Tablespoon rice vinegar

¼ teaspoon black ground pepper

¼ teaspoon oregano

     In medium saucepan over medium heat, sauté onions and garlic in oil until onions are translucent and garlic is tender. Add carrots and sauté an additional 2 minutes. Add carrot, sauce, basil, salt, pepper and oregano. Simmer 20 minutes. Stir in parsley and vinegar. Turn off heat. Let sit 5 minutes before serving.

Makes about 2 cups. Serve over pasta or roasted veggies!

For the Meat Eater: Make meatballs. Put meatballs over their pasta. Spoon spaghetti sauce over the top of meat and pasta.

Black Bean Sweet Potatoes

Sweeeeet and spicay. Oh yeah – bring it on!!

4 large sweet potatoes, washed well (do not peel)

1/2 cup onion, diced

1 1/2 teaspoons. olive oil

1/2 cup Roma tomatoes, diced

2 teaspoons garlic, minced

1/2 teaspoons chili powder

1/2 teaspoons ground cumin

1/4 teaspoons salt

1/8 teaspoons freshly ground black pepper

1 - 15 oz. can black beans, rinsed, and drained

1 - 8 oz. can tomato sauce

hot pepper sauce, to taste

Using a fork, pierce the skins of the sweet potatoes in several places. Place an oven-proof rack on a cookie sheet and place the sweet potatoes on the rack.

Bake at 400 degrees for 60-75 minutes or until the sweet potatoes feel soft when gently squeezed. While the sweet potatoes are baking, prepare the black bean chili. In a medium saucepan, sauté the onion in the olive oil for 3 minutes to soften. Add the green pepper and sauté an additional 3-4 minutes or until the vegetables are tender. Add the tomatoes, garlic, and seasonings, and sauté an additional 2 minutes. Add the black beans, tomato sauce, and season to taste with hot pepper sauce, stir well to combine, and simmer the chili for 10 minutes. Taste and adjust seasonings, to taste.

Remove the saucepan from the heat. When the sweet potatoes are tender, remove the cookie sheet from the oven and leave the sweet potatoes on the rack to cool for 5 minutes. For each serving, place one sweet potato on a plate or in a bowl, split it open, ladle some of the black bean chili over the top, and serve.

Serves 4

For the Meat Eater: Separate out appropriate amount of black bean chili into another pot. Brown ground beef, drain and add to chili mixture.

Jambalaya

"Jambalaya, Crawfish Pie, Fillet Gumbo, 'cause tonight I'm gonna see my ma cher amio..."

1 - 8 oz. pkg. multigrain tempeh

1/4 cup olive oil, divided

2 Tablespoons Creole Seasoning, divided

2 Tablespoons tamari or soy sauce

1 1/2 cups onion

1 cup celery, diced

1 cup red pepper, de-stemmed, deseeded, and diced

1 jalapeno, de-stemmed, deseeded, and diced

1 1/2 cups basmati rice, rinsed

2 Tablespoons garlic, minced

2 cups vegetable stock or water

2 cups tomato, diced (or 1 - 14 oz. can diced tomatoes)

1 teaspoon salt

1 - 15 oz. can red beans, drained, and rinsed

1/2 cup green onion, thinly sliced

1/4 cup freshly chopped parsley

Using your fingers, crumble the tempeh into small pieces onto a plate. In a large pot, sauté the tempeh in 2 tablespoons olive oil for 5 minutes.

Sprinkle 1 Tablespoon Creole Seasoning over the tempeh and sauté an additional 1 minute. Add the tamari, stir well to coat the tempeh, and continue to cook an additional 2-3 minutes or until the liquid has evaporated. Transfer the tempeh to a plate and set aside.

In the same pot, sauté the onion, celery, red pepper, and jalapeno in the remaining 2 Tablespoons olive oil for 5 minutes to soften. Add the rice and garlic, stir well to combine, and continue to cook an additional 2-3 minutes or until the rice turns opaque. Add the vegetable stock, tomatoes, remaining Creole Seasoning, bay leaf, and salt, and bring the mixture to a boil.

Cover, reduce the heat to low, simmer for 20-25 minutes or until the rice is tender and most of the liquid is absorbed. Remove the lid, add the reserved tempeh and remaining ingredients, stir well to combine, and recover the pot. Remove the pot from the heat and let sit for 10 minutes to allow the flavors to blend.

Can be served as a side dish, main dish, or as a filling for wraps or sandwiches.

For the Meat Eater: Separate their portion into another pot and throw in some frozen shrimp and pre-cooked polish sausage (sliced). Cook another 5-10 minutes or until shrimp are fully cooked.

Mexican Skillet

Soooo easy and sooo delish! What a dish!!

2 cups cooked white rice

½ onion

1 can vegetarian chili

2 cans of corn

7 oz diced canned tomatoes

½ shredded soy cheddar or pepper jack cheese

½ teaspoon salt

½ teaspoon onion powder

½ teaspoon chipotle

1 Tablespoon oil for frying

In a skillet over medium heat, sauté onion until translucent. Stir in remaining ingredients except "cheese". *Meat eaters dish would be separated into a different casserole dish at this point.* Cook at 350 degrees for 15 minutes. Add "cheese" cook an additional 15 minutes Works well with a salad and nachos or cornbread and a salad.

For the Meat Eater: Sauté 8 oz of polish sausage. When cooked stir into their casserole dish and bake according to the instructions

Hot pockets

This is a REALLY good recipe for your own hot pockets. Use whatever filling you like. We often use leftover vegi-chili and rice. Sometimes we use leftovers from Mixed Up Lentil Sauce. It is also a good recipe to use if you have meat eaters in the house because they can easily have a meat filling while you have a vegi one. Enjoy!!

2-2 1/4 cups whole wheat flour

1/2 teaspoon baking powder

1 tablespoon sugar

1/4 teaspoon salt

1/3 Cup canola oil

1/2 Cup water

Preheat oven to 375°F.

Lightly oil an aluminum baking sheet or line the baking sheet with parchment paper.

To make the dough, combine the flour, baking powder, sugar, and salt in a mixing bowl. Make a well in the center of the flour and pour in the oil and water. With your hands, work the mixture to form a soft dough, adding more dough if necessary so that it loses its stickiness. Cover dough, set aside and let rest at least 30 min.

Meanwhile, combine the filling ingredients (of choice) and mix well.

Now on a floured surface roll out the prepared dough to 1/16" thickness. Use a 4-5" round cookie cutter or glass to cut out the dough.

Place one heaping teaspoon of the filling on one side of each circle, fold over and pinch edges shut. Use a fork to make the impressions and seal the turnovers.

Arrange the turnovers singly on the prepared baking sheet, bake 15-20 min

For the Meat Eater: Cut luncheon meat or browned ground beef can easily be incorporated into hot pocket.

Sweet Potato Dahl

Oh - what a dahl! A tantalizing mix of sweet and spicy a sweet potato with curry spice!

1 1/2 Tablespoons vegetable oil

1 medium yellow onion, chopped fine

3 cloves garlic, minced

1 1/2 teaspoons curry powder

1/4 teaspoon black pepper

1 cup red lentils, rinsed

2 cups water

2 cups vegetable broth

2 cups peeled, diced sweet potatoes

1 teaspoon salt

In a saucepan, heat the oil. Add the onion and garlic and sauté for 5 minutes. Stir in curry powder, and pepper. Cook for 1 minute more.

Stir in the lentils and water and cook over medium-low heat for 15 minutes, stirring occasionally. Stir in the potatoes and cook for 30 minutes more, stirring occasionally, until the potatoes and lentils are tender. Stir in the salt.

Transfer to a large serving bowl. Serve with Chapattis or flour tortillas. Serves: 4 to 6

For the Meat Eater: This dahl and the chapatti can be their side dish. Goes well with broiled chicken, Cobb salad, or even a roast.

Black Bean Tamale Pie

One hot tamale for your hot tamale.

Polenta Topping

4 cups water

2 cups yellow corn meal or masa

2 teaspoons chili powder

Filling

1 - 14 oz. cans black beans, rinsed and drained

1- 14 oz can of kidney beans, drained and rinsed

1- 14 oz can diced tomatoes with Green Chile – drained

1- 14 oz can of corn - drained

½ teaspoon red pepper

1 teaspoon salt

1 teaspoon oregano

1 teaspoon ground cumin

1 teaspoon garlic powder

1 teaspoon onion powder

4 oz. Tempeh – crumbled

3 Tablespoons olive oil for frying

Preheat oven to 400°F.

In a medium frying pan, sauté tempeh over medium heat for 5 minutes. Add all spices except chili powder. Add beans, stirring and cooking about 3 minutes. Add salsa and reduce heat to a simmer.

Polenta topping: While the bean mixture is simmering, bring 2c water to boil with dash of salt. *A little at a time,* sprinkle the corn meal into the boiling water, stirring constantly to avoid lumps. Continue sprinkling and stirring until you have a thick porridge resembling grits or cream of wheat (The amount of corn meal this takes can vary a little -- don't force all the corn meal into the batter if it looks done with less, you also may have to add more to get a cream of what consistency. If the batter is too thin, add 1 Tablespoon at a time until thickened). Here, Patience really is a virtue!

Remove batter from heat and stir in chili powder. Remove bean mixture from heat. Grease a large baking dish. Spread all of the bean mixture evenly in the dish. Top with polenta batter. Bake at 400°F for 40-45 minutes or until the top corn meal batter is firm to the touch. Let sit 10 minutes before serving. Serve with brown rice and a green salad.

*Tip: to make this recipe a breeze, have your spices pre-measured and ready before you begin.

For the Meat Eater: Make a simple meat sauce to pour over the top. This terrifically tasty dish can easily be topped with hot dog chili with extra ground beef added.

Delish Twice Baked Potato

Restaurant style stuffed potatoes without the price!

1 baked potato

¼ cup veggie crumbles or tofu crumbles or veggies

¼ cup chopped onions

1-2 teaspoons soy margarine

2 Tablespoons hummus

2 Tablespoons salsa

Salt and pepper to taste

(2 Tablespoons imitation bacon bits – optional)

(1/8 cup rice cheese to melt on top –optional)

(This is obviously a meal for one, but can easily be modified to feed a group of people)

Pre-bake your potatoes: Clean the skins, wrap in foil and bake at 350°F for one hour.

Turn oven to broil.

Take pre-baked potato and scrap out the insides with a fork, being careful to keep the potato skins whole, so they look like a bowl and reserve. Place the insides in a bowl, mash with fork and set aside.

Cook onions in pan on medium heat with a little bit of oil or cooking spray. When onions turn transparent add the veggie crumbles. Cook this all until the crumbles are browned and a bit crunchy.

Add this mixture, soy spread, salt and pepper to the mashed potato until well combined. Scoop this mixture into the potato skins, sprinkle the "cheese" and imitation bacon on top. Cook in oven for about 5-10 minutes or until browned, and warm throughout.

When serving, top with hummus and salsa. Serve with soup or salad.

Serves: 1

For the Meat Eater: This makes a wonderful side dish, and would be a treat with a broiled steak.

Chili Nachos

Who can resist a warm plate of chili nachos? This can also be a side dish, but we like it as a main one. It's a great meal for a Friday or Saturday night...or even Thanksgiving!

4 cans of vegetarian chili (separated 2 and 2)- or if you have any leftovers from our "Black Bean and Brown Rice Chili" coming up in a few pages.

½ cup grated rice cheese

¼ cup chopped olives

Optional: jalapenos, banana peppers or other small sliced

Plain Tostada or Nacho chips

Preheat oven to 350°F

In a large pot, heat chili. Meanwhile, lay nachos on a slightly greased baking sheet, top with olives and peppers (if any). Bake at 350°F for 15 minutes.

Top nachos with chili sauce and serve immediately.

For the Meat Eater: Brown ground beef, separate out appropriate amount of chili sauce and mix ground beef in. Serve meat sauce in separate bowl. There will be two bowls of chili sauce at the table, one vegetarian and one meat. Meat-eaters can ladle meat sauce on *their* plate of nachos, and vegetarians can ladle out vegetarian chili sauce onto their plate of nachos.

Quickie Individual Pita Pizzas

Everyone likes their pizza personalized. This recipe gives each family member exactly what they want!

8 Pitas – sliced in half

4-6 oz. Vegetarian spaghetti sauce

1 package of grated rice cheese – mozzarella

Any topping you want. Here are a few ideas:

> caramelized or raw onion,
>
> jalapeno,
>
> garlic,
>
> mushrooms,
>
> Green olives
>
> Pineapples w/ fakin' bacon
>
> spinach
>
> flavored tempeh

Preheat oven to 350°F

Spread spaghetti sauce on back side of pitas. Add desired toppings. Cook for 350°F for 8 minutes, then 550°F for 5 minutes. Serve immediately. Great with slaw and fruit.

Serves 4.

For the Meat Eater: have some pepperoni on hand and top meat eaters pizza with pepperoni as well as desired veggies.

Tortilla Casserole

If you read the ingredient list with your nose close enough to the page, you might just be able to smell it! Mmmm...

2 Tablespoons oil

2 medium onions, chopped

3 cloves garlic, minced

8 oz. chopped canned mushrooms – patted dry

1- 16 oz can refried beans

1 teaspoon chili powder (or more)

1 1/2 teaspoons dried oregano

¼ teaspoon cumin

2 cups tomato purée

1/3 cup silken tofu, pureed in blender

1/3 cup grated soy Parmesan cheese

½ teaspoon salt

8 corn tortillas torn into 2-inch-by-4-inch strips

1/2 cup grated soy cheddar "cheese"

8 ounces salsa

Preheat oven at 375°F

Heat the oil in a pan and add onions and garlic. Stir until transparent. Add the mushrooms, chili powder, cumin and oregano and stir for about 2 to 3 minutes. Add the tomato purée and stir well and bring to boil. Add the pureed tofu and beans, stirring continuously. Stir in the nondairy Parmesan and salt. Add the tortilla strips and stir well.

Pour into a baking dish and sprinkle with the nondairy cheddar cheese. Bake in a preheated oven at 375°F for about 20 minutes, until the "cheese" is slightly browned.

Serve hot with the salsa on the side, soup or salad.

Makes 4 servings

For the Meat Eater: Get saucy!! Brown some ground beef and mix in a canned Enchilada sauce, or ground beef can even be combined with salsa as a spicy sauce. Offer this as topping for casserole.

Bean Burgers

These bean burgers were easy and nummy!

Combine:

1 15 ounce can of pintos - drained and smooshed (like the professional terminology?)

About 1/4 cup cooked white (or brown) rice

3 Tablespoons ketchup

2 Tablespoons mustard

Salt and pepper to taste

Enough bread crumbs to make the mixture "dough like" and thick. Start with 1/3 cup and add as needed

Mix all ingredients together and fry in oil over med to med high heat until they are browned on both sides. Slather additional ketchup, mustard and pickles on your burger buns.

For the Meat Eater: These are quite satisfying, but if a meat dish is required, whip up some hamburgers. At least everyone's buns will look the same!

Garlic Chick Pea Sauce and Jasmine Rice

Love Garlic? Love Garbanzo's? Give this one a try! The aroma will make mouths water.

2 Tablespoons vegetable oil

1 medium onion, chopped

2 large cloves of garlic, minced

1 Tablespoon curry

1 Tablespoon tomato paste

15 oz can of chick peas drained, reserving 3 tablespoon liquid

1/2 tablespoon lemon juice

1 teaspoon salt

1 teaspoon fresh black pepper

¼ teaspoon crushed red pepper, (optional)

1 Tablespoon margarine

Heat oil on medium high heat. Fry onions until slightly browned. Reduce heat to medium. Add garlic, curry, and paste. Stir and simmer about 2 minutes. Add chick peas, liquid, lemon juice, salt, and black pepper. Simmer 5-6 minutes, stirring occasionally. Add red pepper to taste. Add margarine, stirring through to melt it. Stir and simmer for 5 minutes more or until peas are softened and dish is hot. Serve over jasmine rice.

For the Meat Eater: Same as above, just add meat or serve alongside a meat dish!

Chipotle Rice and Lentils (Crock-Pot)

This is a crock-pot recipe, which means, start it, and leave it. I love crock-pot meals, because I can go play and come home and have dinner made! The smoky taste of chipotle is so luscious and unique!

1 cup long-grained rice

1 Tablespoon chipotle powder

3 1/4 cups water

1/4 cup lentils

3 vegetable bouillon cubes

1/2 teaspoon garlic powder

1/4 teaspoon pepper

1 medium onion, quartered and thinly sliced

Combine all the ingredients in a slow cooker. Cover and cook on low for 4 to 5 hours.

Makes about 4 servings

For the Meat Eater: Brown ground beef (or kielbasa) seasoned with chipotle and toss in the meat eaters serving

Sweet Potato Curried Soup

Oh yeah!!!!!!!!!!!!!!!!!! This is sweet and curried with just the right depth. Enjoy!!

1 small onion -chopped

1 garlic clove - chopped

oil for frying

1 small-medium sweet potato - chopped

3 cups vegetable stock

1/2c dried lentils

1 teaspoon curry powder

3/4 teaspoon salt

3/4 teaspoon black pepper

1 5.5-oz can coconut milk

Sauté onion and garlic until onion is translucent. Add remaining ingredients except coconut milk and simmer about 20-25 minutes. Add coconut milk. Puree 1/2 soup in blender or hand mixer and return to pot.

Wonderful with fresh bread or rice and a salad. Excellent with coconut muffins (later in this book)

For the Meat Eater: Broil each a chicken breast with sliced pineapple on top. This will go well with their "side" of soup and coconut muffins.

Eggplant Pomodoro over Angel Hair Pasta

The Olive Garden will come knocking on your door for the recipe...

1 eggplant (sliced into 1/2 inch rounds)

3 Roma tomatoes, diced

10-15 chopped basil leaves, fresh

1 cup vegan mayonnaise (not fat free)

1/4 cup mustard

1 cup breadcrumbs

2 cloves garlic, crushed

1 teaspoon extra virgin olive oil

Pre-heat oven to 400°F.

Combine mayonnaise and mustard in a bowl until well blended. Coat each slice of eggplant with the mayo/mustard mixture and second-coat each slice with vegan breadcrumbs. Arrange coated eggplant slices on foil covered cookie sheet and bake at 400°F degrees for 45 minutes.

While eggplant is baking, sauté diced tomatoes and basil in olive oil until well-heated, and set aside.

Serve baked eggplant with a generous portion of tomato mixture. Enjoy! Serves: 2-4

Preparation time: 30-60 minutes

For the Meat Eater: Serve with a large Chef Salad.

General Tao's Tofu

All the General Tao's you love with none of the chemicals or fat! What more could we ask for?

1 box firm tofu

Egg substitute for 1 egg

1/3 c corn starch

Vegetable oil for frying

5 chopped green onions

1/4 teaspoon ground ginger

1 teaspoon garlic powder

2/3 cup vegetable stock

2 Tablespoons soy sauce

1 packet sweet and low

Cayenne pepper to taste

1 Tablespoons white vinegar

2-4 cups cooked rice

Drain, cut and dry tofu into 1" chunks

Mix egg replacer and water as specified on box. Add additional 3T water. Dip tofu in egg-water mix and coat completely. Spread cornstarch evenly on all sides of tofu. Fry coated tofu in oil until golden brown. Heat oil in pan and fry green onions. Add to tofu.

Add vegetable stock, soy, sweet and low, cayenne and vinegar. In separate bowl make a slur with 1T corn starch and 2T cold water Mix into vegetable stock mix. Add to tofu and onion mixture. Will thicken as it boils.

Serve immediately with steamed rice and veggies.

For the Meat Eater: Batter some boneless skinless chopped chicken breast pieces as you did the tofu. Cook the same way. You will have two dishes: General Tao's Tofu and General Tao's Chicken.

Sloppy Joes

We love these!

3 Tablespoons of margarine

1/2c finely chopped onion

1 lb firm tofu - patted dry and mashed

6 Tablespoons ketchup

3 Tablespoons chili powder

¾ teaspoon salt

¼ teaspoon pepper

4 burger buns – lightly toasted

Heat margarine in skillet over medium heat. Add onion and sauté until onion is translucent. Add mashed tofu and sauté another 10 minutes. Add ketchup, chili powder, salt, and pepper. Heat an additional 10 minutes over low heat. Spoon onto burger buns. This is great with salad or slaw.

Serves 4.

For the Meat Eater: Either add meat to their salad, or brown ½ lb of ground beef, separate out appropriate amount of Sloppy Joe sauce and add ground beef to it.

Garlic, Basil and Artichoke pasta

This would be one of those recipes we could eat daily and be happy as a cat snuggling in a sunbeam!

12 oz of dry linguine

3 garlic cloves - chopped

3 Tablespoons olive oil (divided)

1 grape tomato - chopped

1/2 cup of cooked artichokes

(Either frozen ones that you have cooked, or the canned/marinated variety)

1/4 teaspoon dried oregano

1/2 teaspoon salt

1/2 teaspoon pepper

1/8 cup dried basil

(Grated vegan "parmesan" cheese to top – optional)

If using frozen artichoke hearts, cook according to instructions, then marinate in 2T olive oil, 1/4t garlic 1/4t basil for at least 20 minutes before adding to frying pan.

Boil pasta according to instructions. Meanwhile in a fry pan, heat oil and sauté garlic. When garlic is cooked, add artichokes and tomato. Stir-fry for 2 minutes, then add oregano, salt, pepper and basil. Toss ingredients with linguine and additional tablespoon of olive oil. Serve with a big slice of garlic bread –

For the Meat Eater: Boil some shrimp or scallops. Separate out their portion on pasta and toss with shrimp or scallops.

Mixed Up Lentil Sauce

If we had to pick only one meal to eat daily, this would be it. A sane and tasty meal in this mixed up world.

1 cup mixed lentils

2 Tablespoons olive oil for frying

1 onion – chopped

2 large cloves of garlic – minced

3 cups vegetable broth

2 grape tomatoes – chopped

¼ cup chopped cauliflower

¼ teaspoon cinnamon

¼ teaspoon pepper

½ teaspoon salt

Cook lentils in 3 cups of broth until softened. Set aside. In saucepan over medium-high heat, sauté onions and garlic together until onions are translucent, stirring often. Add cauliflower and sauté for another 3-4 minutes. Add cooked lentils, tomatoes, cinnamon, salt, and pepper. Simmer until warmed all the way through. Puree ½ of mixture in blender until smooth and return to pot.

Simmer 15 minutes and serve over rice, veggies or with chapattis and a salad.

For the Meat Eater: Serve lentil sauce over basic meatballs with chapattis or salad

See-Food Chowder

This is wonderful and richly satisfying.

1 large onion ½ lb extra firm tofu, cubed

1 Tablespoons olive oil

2 teaspoons soy sauce

1 large carrot chopped

½ teaspoons powdered kelp (this helps to give this dish it's salty/ocean flavor!

2 cups vegetable stock ½ teaspoons ground black pepper

2 large baking potatoes – chopped

1 Tablespoons olive oil

1 teaspoon dried thyme

1 cup "milk"

½ teaspoon salt

¼ cup faux bacon bits

½ teaspoon black pepper

    In medium soup pot over medium heat, sauté onions until translucent. Add carrots, sauté another 5 minutes. Add stock, potatoes, thyme salt and pepper. Bring to a boil, then reduce heat. Cover with lid and simmer 15-20 minutes. While soup simmers, in a skillet over medium-high heat, fry oil, soy sauce, pepper, kelp and tofu until tofu is browned and crispy. Once cooked, set aside.

Pour soup into blender and puree until all the soup is smooth. Return mixture to pot. Add "milk" and tofu. Reheat. Serve with garnish of bacon bits.

Great with a loaf of fresh bread, oyster crackers, or chips and a salad.

For the Meat Eater: This one is easy. Grab some frozen clams or scallops; separate the "meat-eater's" soup into a different pot. Toss in the seafood and cook an extra 10 minutes (or until seafood is fully cooked)

Black Bean and Brown Rice Chili (Crock-Pot)

"MMMMMMmmm" (must be said with a strong southern accent) "This is GOOD EATIN!!" Wish ya'll could smell the pot a cookin'! We love Crock-pot recipes – while we're away the cook will stay!

2 - 15oz cans of black beans -drained

1 -14oz can crushed tomatoes - with juice

1/2 cup uncooked brown rice

1/2 cup vegetable broth

1/2 cup coffee

1 cup water

1 teaspoon onion powder

1 teaspoon garlic powder

1/4 teaspoon ground cumin

1/2 teaspoon dried oregano

1 teaspoon ground chipotle

Warm flour tortillas for serving

Put all ingredients in the crock pot, mix well. Cook on low 6-8 hours. Can be served as burritos or in soup bowls with a side of warm "buttered" tortillas.

MMMmmmmm!!!!

For the Meat Eater: Brown some ground beef, Separate out half the soup (or appropriate amount for your family) and mix the browned ground beef in. If you brown the ground beef while the soup is cooking, this will not add to your cooking time. It will only add another pot to clean.

Mexican Black Eyed Peas

This is good stuff! It takes just a minute to prepare but is delish. Best the next day mixed with rice. Also can be served with cornbread and slaw.

14 oz. can black-eyed peas - drained

14oz can diced tomatoes - (We like the green chili ones)

Combine peas and tomatoes in pot. Simmer over low-medium heat 15-20 minutes. Serve with rice or slaw. The peas give a creamy almost nutty flavor to the dish.

For the Meat Eater: Brown ground beef. Separate their portion out and mix the ground beef in with the beans and tomatoes. If they like it really spicy, throw in a jalapeno when you brown the beef. Whooo-ie

Buffalo Tempeh

Miss Buffalo wings?? Try buffalo tempeh!

Cut tempeh into six 1/4" slices

Put slices in bowl with 3T hot sauce. Stir well until they are coated. Let them marinate at least 30 min.

Melt vegan margarine in pan and pan fry tempeh until golden brown. Eat as is or serve in a sandwich or with some hot dipping sauce.

These can be a side, but excellent as a main course with pasta or rice and soup or salad.

For the Meat Eater: Use the same sauce on chicken wings. Cook and serve with the same sides you are eating

Refried Bean Chimichangas

This is sinfully good. Did we mention how tasty this dish is???

1 can vegetarian refried beans

3 Tablespoons chopped olives

1/4 medium onion chopped

1/2 tomato - chopped

Oil for frying

2 flour tortillas - each cut in half, making a total of four

1/2 cup grated vegan cheese for topping - optional. (Beth likes it without)

Sauté onion in a few tablespoons of oil. When translucent add the tomatoes and olives. While that is cooking spread a heavy layer of refried beans on one side of each tortilla shell. Scoop olives, onion and tomato from pan evenly onto each of the four shells. Roll up and use refried beans to act as a seal. Fry in remaining oil on med-med high heat until golden brown. Turn often making sure each side becomes a crisp golden brown color.

Remove from oil, garnish with cheese or salsa if desired.

Apple Yummies (see other recipe) for dessert - goes well with this meal.

For the Meat Eater: Meat eating members of Beth's family will actually eat this one without adding meat, but if needed, brown some ground beef, (or if you feel like making a roast, you can use pulled beef). Put cooked and drained beef in a separate bowl. Beef can easily be added to meat eaters chimichangas.

The Beautiful Pot

This soup is SOOOOoooooOOOO good. It is lovingly adapted from Sarah's Chili in *How it all Vegan*. If you need a good vegetarian/vegan cookbook, we suggest any of Sarah Kramer's books. Yum!!

This soup has a different flavor and less "kick" then Sarah Kramer's. It has become a favorite and we often use this for my hot pocket filling. You really must check out the original version of this chili in *How it all Vegan.*

1 medium onion, chopped

2 medium carrots, chopped

1 Tablespoons olive oil

3 ½ cups canned kidney beans

1-28oz can diced tomatoes

10 oz tomato paste

2 ½ cups canned chickpeas

1 small can chopped mushrooms

1-12oz can of corn

1/2 cup rice (pre cooked)

1 Tablespoons chili powder

1 Tablespoons curry powder

1/2 teaspoon salt

1/2 teaspoon cinnamon

2 1/2 cups vegetable stock

Sauté onions and carrots in oil until onions are translucent. Put in soup pot with remaining ingredients. Simmer 40-60 minutes. Serve with fresh bread. Tastes even better the next day and freezes well. Great with Sweet Potato Fries.

For the Meat Eater: Serve with hot dogs.

Vegan 'Cheese' Lasagna

Why do all the veggie recipes for lasagna have spinach or eggplant in them??

I like a good simple "cheese" lasagna myself - thank you. Here is my "secret" recipe for "cheese" lasagna. SOOOOOOO good!! Even tofu haters LOVE this. This recipe makes 2 loaf pans. Enjoy!

1 lb extra firm tofu (squeeze out the extra water you can by hand)

1/4 cup water

2 teaspoons dried oregano

3 teaspoons dried basil

3 Tablespoons lemon juice

3 Tablespoons garlic powder

1 teaspoons salt

1/4 teaspoons black pepper

1 small onion - chopped (optional)

4 cups tomato sauce

2 cups grated rice cheese for topping (rice cheese looks and tastes more authentic in this recipe then soy cheese)

Lasagna noodles (I cook 12 noodles for 2 pans, 6 noodles if I am halving the recipe)

Cook noodles according to box.

Preheat oven to 350°F. Spray loaf pans with non stick cooking spray. In blender mix tofu, water, oregano, basil, salt, pepper, lemon juice, and garlic powder. Blend until ricotta cheese-like consistency.

In loaf pan, layer noodles, sauce, tofu mixture, rice cheese. Then add another layer of noodles, sauce, tofu mixture and rice cheese. In the top layer, add noodles, sauce and rice cheese. Bake 30 minutes. Let cook 10-15 minutes before serving.

Tip: Use a pie slicer to get beautiful, clean slices of lasagna out of the pan.

For the Meat Eater: Serve with a Cobb salad.

Garden Light Pasta

When Beth was in the process of returning to her vegetarian roots, her good friend Trin supplied her with some great recipes. There were two recipes she could not choose between, and, when you have two good things - why not combine them- you know??

A great meal on days you just want something light and fresh!

2 servings of thin spaghetti (cooked according to directions)

1/4 cup chopped parsley

2 green onions - chopped

1 tomato- chopped

Small yellow squash - chopped

1 small can of mushrooms - sliced

2 Tablespoons vegetable oil for frying

1 Tablespoons sesame oil

2 Tablespoons rice vinegar

1 Tablespoons lemon juice

Salt and pepper to taste

Drain and toss with sesame oil. In a large non stick skillet, heat oil and stir fry onions, parsley, and squash until bright in color - about 1-2 minutes. Then add mushroom and tomato. Stir-fry for another 2 minutes. Toss in pasta and add lemon and vinegar, salt and pepper. Stir-fry for 5 min. Serve hot.

For the Meat Eater: Boil some frozen salad size shrimp. Toss in lemon garlic sauce and toss into their personal portions.

Not the Vindaloo Sauce

This is ROCKIN! Despite the fact that it was Beth's first attempt at Vindaloo sauce and in that way was a complete failure. But, it was a total success in the taste dept. TOTAL.

Can't describe to you what it tastes like - except SO ENTIRELY WONDERFUL!! I wish ya'll could smell this. You can – make some!!

1/2 large onion - finely chopped

3 cloves of garlic - finely chopped

3T vegetable oil for frying the onion and garlic

1 1/2 teaspoons curry powder

1/4 teaspoon ginger

1/2 teaspoon mustard powder

1/2 cup soy milk + 1/4 coconut flavoring [Substituting 1/2c coconut milk would be excellent too]

1/4 cup rice vinegar

1/8 cup tamari

14.5 ounce can diced tomatoes - pureed in the blender

1 teaspoon salt

1 teaspoon chili powder

1/2 teaspoon ground cayenne pepper

1/4 teaspoon black pepper

Sauté onion and garlic in oil until onion is translucent. Add tomato puree, soy milk + coconut flavor and the vinegar. Then stir in the tamari and the rest of the ingredients. Simmer over low heat about 30 minutes for flavors to blend. Serve this over rice and garbanzo beans with a side salad. Spicy and Delish!! Can also be served with chapattis.

For the Meat Eater: Broil some white fish. It will take you only a few extra minutes and they can enjoy "Not the Vindaloo" Sauce as a topping for both their fish and the rice or chapattis. They'll love it.

Veggie Pot Pie

Even the meat eaters in our families l-o-v-e-d this one!!

2 frozen (thawed) pie shells -one for the top, one for the bottom or, if you've got the time, make your own: Recipe to follow

1/2 onion - chopped

1 potato-chopped

2 cans vegan 'cream of' mushroom soup

16 oz bag frozen veggies (peas/carrots/corn/lima - mix), steamed

bag of grated rice cheese

3 Tablespoons chopped olives

1 small can mushrooms

Garlic powder, chili powder, onion powder, salt and pepper to taste

Precook bottom crust 10 min. at 400°F

To steamed veggies add spices, and soup. Combine thoroughly. Layer 1/2 cheese on bottom crust. Spoon veggie mix over crust and cheese. Top veggie mix with other 1/2 of cheese. Put other crust on top, and close up Bake at 400°F for 45 minutes.

Let sit 10 minutes before serving.

For the Meat Eater: Either a) compliment this dish with hot dogs or broiled chicken or b) if you're feeling kind and energetic, make a separate pie with the same ingredients as above but with added cooked chicken.

Easy Vegan Pie Crust

2 cups flour

1 1/2 tbsp sugar

1/2 tsp salt

1/2 cup plus 2 tbsp vegan margarine

2 tbsp vegetable oil

3 tbsp cold water

    Combine the flour, sugar and salt in a large bowl. Cut in the vegan margarine. Mix until crumbly. In a separate bowl, whisk together oil and water, then add to flour mixture, mixing just until a dough forms. Cover the dough with plastic wrap. Chill for 30 minutes.

    Roll out onto a lightly floured surface to about 1/4 inch thickness and gently press into a pie tin.

Breads and Sides

Even vegans love their sides. And bread is not taboo.

Sweet Potato Fries and Other Stories

Curried Sweet Potato Fries

YUM! Try these for a change. Go ahead, consider it a dare...

1 large sweet potato - scrubbed and cleaned (skin on)

1T Olive oil

2t curry powder

1/4t salt

       Preheat oven to 425°F. Cut potato into 1/4 inch strips. Mix olive oil, curry and salt. Roll strips in the curry oil. Place greased baking sheet. Bake for 15 minutes, then turn and bake another 15 minutes.

Uber good!

* If you're going to make one investment, we recommend your obtaining a rice cooker. Rice cookers consistently produce quality fluffy rice. Other grains can easily be cooked in them as well.

Vintners Rice

This Beth's favorite rice! "The smell while it is cooking absolutely makes my mouth water." .

2 Tablespoons margarine

½ medium onion – finely chopped

Dash of black pepper

1 cup basmati white rice

2 cups vegetable broth (or 2 cups water with 2 vegetable broth cubes)

2/3 teaspoon salt

Place margarine in bottom of 3 quart pan. Add rice and remaining ingredients. Bring to a boil. Cover and simmer for 20 minutes, until all water is dissolved. Remove from heat. Let sit 5 minutes and serve.

Mexican Rice

If we had to choose one "staple" Mexican rice, this would be it. Make this one and build your meal around it.

1 Tablespoon olive oil

1 Tablespoon onion powder

1 teaspoon garlic powder

1 ½ teaspoons chili powder

½ teaspoon salt

1 cup basmati white rice

2 cups vegetable broth (or 2 cups water with 2 vegetable broth cubes)

Place oil in the bottom of 3 quart pan. Add rice and remaining ingredients. Bring to a boil, cover and simmer for 20 minutes, until all water is dissolved. Remove from heat. Let sit 5 minutes and serve.

Whole Wheat Chapattis

These taste authentic and the dough is beautiful!! They are so easy to make if you remember one thing - once you roll them out, fry them right away! Chapattis are an Indian bread usually served with Dahl or another lentil dish. Traditionally white flour is used, but I'm a health nut - what can I say?

1 1/2 cups whole wheat flour

1/2 teaspoon salt

2 Tablespoons oil

3/4 cup water

In ceramic or glass bowl, combine flour, salt and oil. Slowly add water until you get a nice workable dough. Knead for 5 minutes. Cover for about an hour. Pull apart into 10 sections. Roll each section into balls. Roll each ball into at least a 6" circle. Fry on dry skillet over med-high heat until *lightly browned* on both sides. Yum!

Serve with any dahl or soup.

Luscious Coconut Muffins

Yum!! They are delicious and will give a bit extra fiber. For a lighter muffin, use unbleached flour or even (gasp) white flour.

1/2 cup unsweetened coconut

1 cups unbleached flour

1 1/2 teaspoons baking powder

1/4 teaspoon salt

1/2 cup soy milk

1 1/2 teaspoon Ener-G Ener-G Egg Replacer : mixed as directed

2 Tablespoons water

2 Tablespoons vegetable oil

1/4 cup Splenda brown sugar blend

1/2 teaspoon vanilla

Preheat the oven to 350°F.

In a bowl, combine the dry ingredients, including toasted coconut. In a separate bowl, mix together the wet ingredients. Add wet ingredients to dry ingredients, and stir until blended. Pour into a lightly greased bread pan, and bake until a toothpick comes out clean and loaf is lightly browned (about 20 minutes for a loaf or 15 minutes muffins). Remove from pan, and cool on a wire rack. Excellent with Sweet Potato Curried Soup in the entrees section of the book

Serves: 1 mini loaf or 12 mini muffins

The BEST Hummus!!

It's the best hummus. Need we say more?

1/2 Tablespoon ground garlic

2 Tablespoons olive oil

2 cups cooked chick peas

1 Tablespoon fresh parsley - chopped

3 Tablespoons + 1 teaspoon lemon juice

1/4 cup tahini

1 teaspoon salt

1/3-1/2 cup water (added to blender slowly)

Mix garlic, olive oil, parsley, lemon juice, tahini and salt in a bowl. Add cooked chick peas to the bowl. Pour into blender. Blend on' puree' slowly adding the water until the consistency you want is achieved. Refrigerate until chilled.

Fava Bean Dip

What a luscious dip this is. Make sure your family eats it too - then they won't notice the garlic on your breath!

3 cloves of garlic – minced

2 Tablespoons chopped parsley

1 Tablespoon olive oil

1-14 oz can Fava beans – drained

1 teaspoon salt

1 Tablespoon lemon juice

¼ teaspoon black pepper

In small skillet sauté the garlic and parsley in olive oil until garlic is tender. In separate bowl, mash fava beans with a potato masher. Add mashed beans and remaining ingredients into skillet. Heat another 5 minutes. Good warm or room temperature. Great with chapattis or pitas.

A Little Something For The Sweet Tooth.

Vegan Cheesecake

And you thought you'd never have cheesecake again!

1 block extra firm, drained

1/2 cup plain soymilk

1/2 cup sugar

1 Tablespoon vanilla

1 Tablespoon lemon juice

1/4 cup sugar free maple syrup

1 vegan graham cracker pie crust

Preheat oven to 350°F.

Combine all ingredients (except crust, of course) into a blender and blend until creamy. Pour this blended mixture into graham cracker crust. Bake at 350°F. for 30 minutes. Put in refrigerator or freezer until cool.

Mom's Chocolate Chip Cookies

these are cookies to be adored. The vegan version is below.

2 1/4 cup all purpose flour

1 teaspoon baking soda

1/2 teaspoon salt

1 cup softened vegan margarine

1/4 cup Splenda sugar blend

1/2 cup Splenda brown sugar blend

2 teaspoon vanilla extract

2 egg replacers

2 cup vegan chocolate chips

1 cup chopped pecans

Preheat oven to 375°F. Stir flour, soda and sugar together. Set aside. I n bowl, using electric mixer (low speed) beat margarine, sugar and vanilla until creamy. Add egg replacer. Mix on low speed until incorporated. Gradually blend dry mix into creamy mix. Stir in chocolate chips and nuts. Drop by tablespoons onto ungreased cookie sheets. Bake 9-11 minutes or until golden brown.

Super Easy Coconut Cookies

Mmmm...Coconutty and Sweet and moist.

It's a recipe I've been playing with. Coconut lovers gave this version rave reviews.

1/2 cup Splenda brown sugar blend

1 Tablespoon vanilla

3/4 margarine

1 cup coconut

1/4 cup soy milk

1 3/4 cup quick oats

Melt margarine and stir in sugar. Add soy milk. Bring to a boil over medium heat for 2 minutes - stirring constantly. Remove from heat. Add remaining ingredients and mix well. Drop by tablespoons onto wax paper. Let cool before eating. Especially good from the refrigerator.

Guilt Free Pudding - can it be??

Get your sweet fix and your protein fix with virtually no sugar - no way! This is too good to be true.

1 package soft tofu

2 Tablespoons liquid sweetener

1/4 cup vegetable oil

1/4 cup sugar

1/4 cup sugar free "maple syrup"

2 1/4 teaspoons vanilla

1/4 teaspoons salt

Optional: 3 Tablespoons cocoa powder

Mix all ingredients in blender, puree until pudding consistency. Refrigerate 30 minutes before serving.

Apple Yummies

Here they are! Great for cool evenings of Autumn.
Mmmmm..... or a picnic in the summer!

2 burrito shells each cut in half to make four

1 granny smith apple, peeled and cubed

1 teaspoon sugar

1 packet sweet and low

1 teaspooon cinnamon

Karo syrup to seal shells

Oil for frying

Distribute cubed apples and spices evenly between all
four shells. Roll up tightly and seal ends with syrup. Fry in oil
over medium - medium high heat, turning so all sides become
golden brown. Delish!!

Bi-Polar Cake

This little number can be vanilla or chocolate – whatever you mood. Put in the cocoa, leave it out. This can be made into muffins by pouring the batter into a muffin tin, or a cake by pouring the batter into a cake pan. Vanilla-Chocolate, Muffins-Cake? So many choices...

3 cups flour

2 cups sugar

6 Tablespoons cocoa (optional: Add for a chocolate cake or omit for a vanilla one)

2 teaspoons baking soda

1 teaspoon salt

2 cups of water

¾ cup vegetable oil

2 Tablespoons white vinegar

2 teaspoons vanilla

1 cup chocolate chips

Preheat oven to 350°F. Mix dry ingredients in a large bowl first. Stir in wet ingredients. Mix until there are no lumps. Stir in chocolate chips. Pour into cake pan and bake approximately 40 minutes or until toothpick comes out of center clean.

Pumpkin Pie

Now you can eat pie! Pumpkin pie! Have pumpkin pie whenever you want. Be daring and don't wait until Thanksgiving!!

1 ½ cups soy milk

Egg replacer equal to 2 eggs

1 – 16 oz can of pumpkin

1/3 cup Splenda brown sugar blend

1 teaspoon cinnamon

½ teaspoon powdered ginger

1 teaspoon vanilla

¼ teaspoon allspice

1 vegan 9" pie crust

      Preheat oven to 350°F. In large bowl, whisk milk and egg replacer together. Add pumpkin and spices. Pour into pie crust and bake for about 35-45 minutes until a toothpick inserted in the center comes out clean. Cool before serving.

Quick 'n EZ Vegan S'mores

Same ooey-gooey chocolaty goodness...just vegan

vegan graham crackers

vegan marshmallow – yes they exist. Try Sweet and Sara's in the refrigerator section of many health food stores.

vegan chocolate chips or dark chocolate bar (62%+ cocoa)

You know the drill. Cut one marshmallow and place each half on a graham cracker. Sprinkle with chocolate chips or small pieces of chocolate bar. Cover gently with another graham cracker. Wrap in aluminum foil. Cook in toaster oven for 4-5 minutes on 350°F. Since each toaster oven is different, stay nearby. You don't want anything to burn. Carefully unwrap.

Other easy vegan treats:

Celery with any nut butter sprinkled with vegan chocolate chips/raisins

Apples with peanut butter

Shredded raw yam with raisins and chopped apple sprinkled with cinnamon.

Staples for your Vegan Kitchen

With these on hand, you will be able to make many of the recipes in this book. If you don't have something a recipe calls for, look in your cabinet. Improvise! Improvise!

All manner of vegetables: canned, frozen, but especially fresh – and organic if you can.

Canned and dried beans

Dried beans and lentils

Spices

Egg-less Mayonnaise

Pie Crusts

Vegetable Broth

Imitation Bacon Bits

Egg Replacer

Molasses

Pasta

Nuts and Seeds

Vanilla Extract

Dried fruit, especially dates and raisins

Garlic Cloves

Peanut Butter

Vegetarian baked beans

Tomato sauce

Bran

Tofu / Tempeh / Miso paste

Soy and/or Rice Cheese

Sesame Oil / Tahini

Cocoa Powder

Olive Oil

Soy and Rice Milk

Sugar

Splenda Brown Sugar Blend

Vegan Cream of Mushroom Soup

Lemon Juice

Dairy Free Margarine

Brown Rice

Yeast

Flour

Masa or Cornmeal

Fresh Fruit (freeze bananas for smoothies)

Bread Crumbs

Quick Oats

Flour and CornTortillas

CONVERSIONS

1 tablespoon (T) = 3 teaspoons (t)

1/16 cup = 1 Tablespoon

1/8 cup = 2 Tablespoons

1/6 cup = 2 Tablespoons + 2 teaspoons

1/4 cup = 4 Tablespoons

1/3 cup = 5 Tablespoons + 1 teaspoon

3/8 cup = 6 Tablespoons

1/2 cup = 8 Tablespoons

2/3 cup = 10 Tablespoons + 2 teaspoons

3/4 cup = 12 Tablespoons

1 cup = 48 teaspoons

1 cup = 16 Tablespoons

8 fluid ounces (fl oz) = 1 cup

APPENDIX

{Information compiled from United States Department Agriculture's Food Safety and Inspection Service Recall Archives and individual Recall Releases via its website www.fsis.usda.gov}

Recall Case Archive - 2009

Product, reason	Date Recall Initiated	Pounds recalled
Smoked Beef Brisket Product (*Listeria*)	Aug 24, 2009	207
Marcacci Meats Ground Beef Products (*E. coli*)	Aug 17, 2009	128
Frozen Meat and Poultry Products - Perogies (unapproved ingredient)	Jun 30, 2009	208,768
Sausage Product (undercooked)	Jun 24, 2009	350
Cameco, Inc. Ready-to-Eat Meat and Poultry Products, various (under processing)	Jun 5, 2009	79,312

Duck Leg Confit; Hungarian Brand Kolbase (*Listeria*)	Jun 3, 2009	564
SP Provisions Ground Beef Products (*E. coli*)	Jun 2, 2009	39,973
XL Four Star Beef, Beef Products (not presented for reinspection for import into US from Canada)	May 26, 2009	14,560
Paisano Meat Beef and Pork Products (undeclared sulfites)	May 22, 2009	350,000
Wayne Provision Co, Bulk Frozen Pork Sausage Products (undeclared allergen)	May 14, 2009	2,075
AMIGO'S Home Style PORK Tamales Wrapped in Corn Husk (undeclared allergen – Wheat – not on label)	May 14, 2009	4,594
Bob's Food City Ground Beef Products	May 12, 2009	373

(*E. coli*)		
A & G Brand Ground Beef Products (*E. coli*)	May 4, 2009	4,663
Mucci's Food Products, Inc. Frozen Meat and Poultry Pasta Products (adulterated and misbranded)	Apr 26, 2009	(undetermined but reported 30,973 pounds recalled)
Ivar's Soup, Turkey Flavored Egg Noodle Soup Base with Turkey Meat (undeclared allergen)	Apr 17, 2009	37,776
015-2009, Frozen Chicken Products (*Salmonella*)	Apr 4, 2009	12,460
012-2009, Ball Park Brand Beef Franks (mislabeling / allergen)	Mar 25, 2009	1,728
Aidells Smoked Chicken Sausage w/mango and jalapeño pepper	Mar 24, 2009	3,456

(mislabeling/allergen)		
Trader Joe's Chile Lime Chicken Burgers (foreign material)	Feb 27, 2009	13,776
Weis Simply Delicious Chicken Cordon Bleu (undeclared allergen)	Feb 27, 2009	2,852
Wei-Chuan USA Granulated Chicken Bouillon Products (ineligible for import)	Feb 24, 2009	89,531
Alaska Sausage Co. Sausage Products (*Listeria*)	Feb 6, 2009	872
Whitey's™ Frozen, Chili Beef Products (foreign material)	Jan 30, 2009	**676,560**
Barber Foods Frozen, Stuffed Chicken Products (foreign material)	Jan 20, 2009	6,050
Patrick Cudahy Bacon Bit Products (*Listeria*)	Jan 3, 2009	3,590

2008

7-Eleven Fresh to Go Burrito Products (*Listeria*)	Dec 30, 2008	172
Frozen Krakow Sausage (*Listeria*)	Dec 25, 2008	750
Nostrano Sopressata Sausage Products (*Listeria*)	Dec 19, 2008	1 (yes, one)
Dawn International Imported Pork Products (Dioxin)	Dec 11, 2008	33,880
Tommy Moloney's Inc. Imported Pork Products (Dioxin)	Dec 11, 2008	4,041
Rupari Food Services Imported Pork Products (Dioxin)	Dec 11, 2008	41,020
DeNunzio Sausage Products (Undeclared Allergens)	Dec 2, 2008	36,388
Blimpie Frozen Beef Sandwich Products (*Listeria*)	Nov 28, 2008	5,250

John Soules Foods Chicken Products (Undeclared Allergens)	Nov 26, 2008	8,496
Dutch Prime Foods Ground Beef Products (*E. coli*)	Nov 24, 2008	345
Nestlé Lean Cuisine Chicken Meals (Foreign Materials)	Nov 17, 2008	879,565
Zeigler Hot Dog Products (*Listeria*)	Nov 8, 2008	28,610
Barber Foods, Schwan's Frozen Stuffed Chicken Products (Extraneous Material)	Nov 7, 2008	41,415
Jolly Good Sausage Products (Undeclared Allergens)	Nov 1, 2008	600
VT Burger Co. Ground Beef Products (*E. coli*)	Oct 16, 2008	2,758
Packers Provision Beef Trimmings (*E.*	Oct 10, 2008	420

coli)		
A.C.S. Meyners Ltda. Beef Trimmings (*E. coli*)	Oct 8, 2008	20,460
Astro Meats & Seafood, Inc. Beef Trimmings (*E. coli*)	Oct 8, 2008	4,200
Colorado Foods Products Beef Trimmings (*E. coli*)	Oct 8, 2008	2,340
Food Evolution Ready-to-Eat Turkey Burrito Wrap (*Listeria*)	Sep 30, 2008	16..just 16
Hot Pockets Frozen Stuffed Pepperoni Pizza Sandwich Products (foreign material)	Aug 21, 2008	215,660
Simmering Soup, Inc. Chicken Noodle Products (undeclared allergen)	Aug 19, 2008	987
Renna's Meat Market Ground Beef Products	Aug 12, 2008	780

(*E. coli*)		
May's Brand Pork Products (*Listeria*)	Aug 10, 2008	4,535
Beef, Ltd. Beef Products (*E. coli*)	Aug 14, 2008	1.36 MILLION
Dallas City Packing, Inc. *cattle heads* (Prohibited Materials..yeah, that being tonsils that were not completely removed..eeww)	Aug 7, 2008	941,271
S&S Foods Ground Beef Products (*E. coli*)	Aug 6, 2008	153,630
Tyson Foods, Inc. Chicken Breast Products (Undeclared Allergens)	Aug 6, 2008	51,360
Progressive Gourmet Ready-to-Eat Chicken Products (*Listeria*)	Aug 5, 2008	285
Beef Packers, Inc. beef cheek meat (*E. coli*)	Jul 23, 2008	1,560

Lean Pockets Frozen Stuffed Chicken Sandwiches (Plastic)	Jul 14, 2008	199,417
Nebraska Beef, Ltd. Beef Products (*E. coli*) [*Yes* the same company that will recall more beef on August 14, 2008]	Jul 3, 2008	5.3 MILLION
Kroger Ground Beef (*E. coli*)	Jul 3, 2008	UNDETERMINED *but* reported 1,613,122 pounds
Paradise Locker Meats Cattle Heads (Prohibited Materials – more tonsils - eew)	Jun 26, 2008	120
Frontier Meats Cattle Heads (Prohibited Materials)	Jun 26, 2008	2,850
Gourmet Foods, Inc. Chicken Products (*Listeria*)	Jun 9, 2008	130
Dutch's Meats Ground Beef (*E. coli*)	Jun 8, 2008	13,275
Cecina Los Amigos pork blood sausages	May 21,	290

(*Listeria*)	2008	
JSM Meat Holdings Beef Products (*E. coli*)	May 16, 2008	UNDETERMINED but reported 345,000 pounds
Fairbank Reconstruction Corp. Ground Beef Products (plastic)	May 12, 2008	22,481
May's brand Ground Beef Products (*E. coli*)	May 8, 2008	68,670
Gourmet Boutique Meat and Poultry Products (*Listeria*)	May 3, 2008	286,320
Elkhorn Valley Packing Frozen Cattle Heads (prohibited materials: you guessed it...more tonsils)	Apr 4, 2008	406,000
Koch Foods Frozen Chicken Products (mislabeling: frozen, pre-browned and raw but labeled as pre-cooked...oops)	Mar 29, 2008	1,420

Cagle's Inc. Chicken Giblets (adulterated)	Mar 14, 2008	943,000
Gourmet Boutique Meat and Poultry Products (*Listeria*) [these folks again]	Mar 4, 2008	6,970
Discover Cuisine™ Frozen Chicken Entrées (*Listeria*)	Mar 4, 2008	3,780
Discover Cuisine™ Frozen Chicken Entrées (*Listeria*)	Mar 3, 2008	10,368
Discover Cuisine™ Frozen Chicken Entrées (*Listeria*)	Mar 2, 2008	2,184
Hallmark/Westland Beef Products Only(non-ambulatory/ downer cows)* **THIS WAS THE LARGEST BEEF RECALL IN THE US IN HISTORY***	Feb 17, 2008	143,383,823
Chef's Requested Foods Bacon-wrapped Beef Tenderloin Products	Feb 1, 2008	8,910

149

(Undeclared Allergen: soy/milk)		
Perdue Perfect Portions Chicken Products (Undeclared Allergen)	Jan 26, 2008	24,710
Rochester Meat Company Ground Beef Products (*E. coli*)	Jan 12, 2008	188,000
Mark's Quality Meats Ground Beef Products (*E. coli*)	Jan 5, 2008	13,150

BIBLIOGRAPHY

Nestle, Marion. *Food Politics: How the Food Industry Influences Nutrition, and Health, Revised and Expanded Edition (California Studies in Food and Culture)* 2007

Singer, Peter. *In Defense of Animals*, Wiley-Blackwell; First edition September 2, 2005

Singer, Peter, Mason, Jim. *The Ethics of What We Eat: Why Our Food Choices Matter*, Rodale Books, March 6, 2007

Masson, Jeffrey Moussaieff. *The Face on Your Plate: The Truth About Food*, (2009) Jeffrey Moussaieff Masson

Francione, Gary L. *Introduction to Animal Rights: Your Child or The Dog.* Philadelphia: Temple University, 2000.

Regan, Tom. *A Case for Animal Rights*

Stanford, Craig B, Bunn, Henry T. *Meat-eating and Human Evolution.* Oxford University Press. 2001

Stanford, Craig B. *Upright: The Evolutionary Key to Becoming Human* (2003) Houghton Mifflin Company

Schlosser, Eric. *Fast Food Nation: The Dark Side of The All American Meal.* Houghton Mifflin Company. 2001

Spurlock, Morton. *Don't Eat This Book: Fast Food and The Supersizing of America*, Putnam Adult, 2005

Lappe, Frances Moore. *Diet For a Small Planet.* Ballentine Books 1991.

Pimentel, David; Pimentel, Marcia. *Food, Energy and Society.* New York Edward Arnold (Publishers) Ltd. (1979)

Lappe, Frances Moore; Collins, Joseph. *World Hunger: 10 Myths (Every country has the resources to feed its people)*, San Francisco, Institute for Food and Development Policy (1979)

http://earthfirst.com

Physicians Committee for Responsible Medicine
(http://www.pcrm.org)

Fox, Michael Allen. *Deep Vegetarianism*. Temple University Press. (1999)

Eshel Gidon Dr., Martin, Pamela. *Diet, Energy and Global Warming*. Chicago, IL, Department of Geophysical Sciences, University of Chicago (2005)

Interviews
        Animal Voices, "Meat and The Environment" www.animalvoices.ca, CIUT, Toronto, Dr, Gidon Eshel,

Robbins, John. *The Food Revolution: How Your Diet Can Help Save Your Life and Our World*, John Robbins, (2001).

Nemitz, Bill, "*Enough water? Let's Figure It Out*", Portland Press Herald, April 9, 2009

Chuzhao Lin, "Bring Your Lagoon Back to Life", *http://www.proactmicrobial.com/images/Hoardsarticle.pdf*.

John D. Lawrence, Returns from Finishing Feeder Pigs, (File B133, August 2008), *http://www.extension.iastate.edu/ agdm/livestock/html/b1-33.html*.

http://www.fergusonfoundation.org/hbf/cow_in_out/cowmoreinfo.html.

http://www.news.cornell.edu/releases/aug97/livestock.hrs.html

http://ga.water.usgs.gov/edu/wulv.html

JFF. (2008). *programs*. Retrieved from Jewish Helping Hands | Yad Soffin Foundation, Mending the World, one miracle at a time: http://jewishhelpinghands.org

JTA. (2009, March 26). *IDF: One-quarter of Gaza Palestinians killed were civilians*. Retrieved from JTA: The Global News Service of The Jewish

People: http://jta.org/news/article/2009/03/26/1004020/idf-one-quarter-of-gaza-palestinians-killed-were-civillians

www.mfa.gov. (2008, June) *Israel Ministry of Foriegn Affairs*. Retrieved from The Hamas terror war against Israel: http://www.mfa.gov.il/MFA/Terrorism+Obstacle+to+Peace/Palestini an+terror+since+2000/Missile+fire+from+Gaza+on+Israeli+civilian+ targets+Aug+2007.htm.

The Vegan News, *The Company Acts 1944-1976*, Memorandum of Association of The Vegan Society, pp1.

http://www.who.int/hdp/poverty/en/

http://suprememastertv.com/bbs/board.php?bo_table=holidaycard&wr_id=141 &goto_url=&url=link1_0

Tidwell, Mike "The Low-Carbon Diet" Audubon Magazine, January-February 2009.

Bittman Mark, Rethinking-the Meat Guzzler, NY Times. January 27, 2008

FAO Newsroom, "Livestock a major threat to environment" November 29, 2006.

Cees de Haan, Henning Steinfeld, Harvey Blackburn.; "Livestock and the Environment: Finding a Balance" 1997

Rhett A. Butler,"*Deforestation in the Amazon*" http://www.mongabay.com/brazil.html#cattle

"Meat the Truth", Nikolaas G. Pierson Foundation

"Brazil: Amazon Admits Amazon Deforestation on the Rise" Associated Press , August 30, 2008 as sited at http://www.msnbc.msn.com.

Juan Forero, , "Argentine Cattle no longer just home on the Rage", September 14, 2009. Morning Edition, National Public Radio Transcript

Nancy Stoner, "Poisoned Waters", April 20, 2009. *http://switchboard.nrdc.org/blogs/nstoner/poisoned_waters.html*

http://www.happycow.net/health-animal-ingredients.html

"Veal, a Byproduct of the Cruel Dairy industry", http://origin.www.peta.org/mc/factsheet_display.asp?ID=102

United States Department of Environmental Protection's *"Regulatory Definitions of Large CAFOs, Medium CAFOs, Small CAFOs"*

http://www.azstarnet.com/sn/news/283076.php

Danit Lidor, http://www.wired.com/Big Stink Over a Pig, 07.01.02

Scientists Link Influenza A (H1N1) Susceptibility to Common Levels of Arsenic Exposure, Press Release, May 20, 2009.

Steve Wing, Suzanne Wolf, Environmental Health Perspectives, Volume 108, Number 3, March 2000,

"PEW Commission says Industrial Scale Farm Animals Production Poses "Unacceptable" Risks to Public Health, Environment", PEW Charitable Trust Press Release, April 29, 2008. http://www.gaia.com /quotes/neal_barnard#ixzz0T19StUn

http://www.greenpeace.org/usa/news/nike-establishes-policy-072209 Timberlane's blog

http://www.earthkeeper.com/blog/?s=deforestation

"Brazil Retailers Ban Beef from cleared Amazon Area". Reuters, June 12, 2009

Craig WJ. *Nutrition and Wellness. A Vegetarian Way to Better Health*. Golden Harvest Books, Berrien Springs, MI, 1999

Thorogood M, Carter R, et al. Plasma lipids and lipoprotein cholesterol concentrations in people with different diets in Britain. *Br Med J* 1987;295: 351-3.

www.tewskburyodor.org/aboutus.html

www.tewksburyodor.org

Livestock's Long Shadow-Environmental Issues and Options, Food and Agriculture Organization of The United Nations, November 2006, p. 80, .

Chuzhao Lin, "Bring Your Lagoon Back to Life", http://www.proactmicrobial.com/images/Hoards%20article.pdf.

John D. Lawrence, Returns from Finishing Feeder Pigs, (File B133, August 2008),

http://www.extension.iastate.edu/agdm/livestock/html/b1-33.html.

Karl Blankenship. "Large Spring Algae blooms pose array of possibilities" Bay Journal. June 1996

Dr. Bill Chameides, "Predicting Dead Zones" The Green Grok, Nicholas Insider, July 2009,

David Malmquist, "Dead Zones Continue to Spread". August 14, 2008. http://www.vims.edu/newsandevents/topstories/2008-dead-zones-spread.php.

David Perlman. "Scientists Alarmed by Ocean Dead-Zone Growth". San Francisco Chronicle, .August 15, 2008.

http://www.ehponline.org/docs/2000/108-3/focus.html

Fran Weaver, "Baltic Dead Zone Spreading" Helsinki Times, General News, September 1, 2008

http://www.commondreams.org/archive/2008/08/15/11004

http://ga.water.usgs.gov/edu/wulv.html

http://www.news.cornell.edu/releases/aug97/livestock.hrs.html

"Poultry Growers Rattled" Anita Huslin. The Washington Post, July 7, 2003, pB1

www.simplot.com

Roger Luckenbach, PhD, *Fecal Maters – Here's the scoop on poop.* The Poop Sheet, *http://www.plumbingsupply.com/pooppage.html*

http://www.fergusonfoundation.org/hbfcow_in_out/cowmoreinfo.html.

http://www.lasvegasnevada.gov/files/BRO-WPCF_04.pdf

http://michigan.sierraclub.org/issues/greatlakes/articles/cafofacts.html.waste

Cesspool of Shame", National Defense Council, Clean Water Network, July 2001.

Fact Sheet 102-98 - The Chesapeake Bay: Geologic Product of Rising Sea Level". U. S. Geological Survey. 1998-11-18

Ian Urbina, "On Maryland, Focus on Poultry Industry Pollution" New York Times, November 28, 2008

'Dead Zones' Expand in Coastal Waters Around the World, Science In The News". September 8, 2008 Voice Of America Interview Transcript

"Feeding Farmed Fish". Fisheries Committee of the European Parliament,. Federation of European Aquaculture Producers (FEAP) October 2002

Jenkins DJA, Popovich D, Kendall C, et al. Effect of a diet high in vegetables, fruit, and nuts on serum lipids.*Metabolism* 1997;46:530-7

Mian N. Riaz. "Soy Application In Food", p. 12 CRC Press 2006

http://www.soyatech.com/soy_facts.htm

Carolyn Dimitri, Anne Effland. "Milestones in U.S. Farming and Farm Policy", Amber Waves, June 2005. US Department of Agriculture/Economic Research Service

http://www.sciencedaily.com/releases/1997/08/970812003512.htm

http://www.celsias.com/article/dishing-dirt-with-david-montgomery.

http://epa.gov/methane/sources.html

http://www.foodnavigator-usa.com/Product-Categories/Flavors-and-colors/New-labeling-rules-for-cochineal-bug-coloring

Kate Connelley, "Pill stops cow burps and helps save the planet" . The Guardian, March 23, 2007

Executive Summary, 2009 U.S. Greenhouse Gas Inventory Report, April 2009, USEPA

http://www.squidoo.com/vegetarian-quotes

http://www.veganoutreach.org/whyvegan/health.html

Carbon Savings Table US, *www.animalconcerns.org*

U.S. Census Bureau, *http://www.census.gov/ipc/www/idb/worldpopgraph.php*

United States Department Agriculture's Food Safety and Inspection Service Recall Archives and individual Recall Releases via its website *www.fsis.usda.gov*

About The Authors

Beth lives in New England with her husband and two sons. She has published three vegan cookbooks and adores creating scrumptious vegan meals. She looks forward to teach some local vegan cooking classes with her fabulous co-author Susan.

Susan lives in Maine with her hubby, 2 sons, and 2 dogs. When she's not searching for sea glass along Southern Maine's sandy coastline, she's creating new vegan concoctions.